I0138726

Kaos Hieroglyphica
Alchemy for the New Aeon

Anton Channing
(Frater M 1232)

KAOS HIEROGLYPHICA
Alchemy for the New Aeon

©2003 Anton Channing

ISBN 1869928-83-0

ALL RIGHTS RESERVED

No part of this publication may be reproduced, stored in a retrieval system or transmitted in any form or by any means, electronic, mechanical, photocopying, scanning, recording or otherwise without the prior written permission of the author and the publisher.

Cover design and illustration by Anton Channing

Internal illustrations by Anton Channing

This edition published by:
When Illuminated Press
http://www.kiamagic.com/WhIP

In collaboration with:
Mandrake of Oxford
PO Box 250
Oxford
OX1 1AP
United Kingdom

Anton wishes to thank...

The Dead Chaosists Society, The Kaotic and Illuminated Adepts and The Illuminates Of Thanateros, The I∴I∴, The Red Priory, The Illuminati Youth, The Eternal Triangle of Chaos, Colour the Grey, Occulture and everyone else with whom I have worked Sorcery, in any of its many shades and colours...

All the various authors quoted in this work. You should all be in the Bibliography. If you aren't, feel free to complain. All complaints should be sent to Secret Atlantis H.Q., 23 Lemuria Place, New Mu, Atlantis, where they will be promptly ignored.

With Special Thanks to Jaq D. Hawkins for proof reading the original manuscript and for being my inspiration and muse for the latter half of this book. Not to mention writing the forward! I Love You.

Thanks also Chaos itself, for spawning this existence, without which this book would not have been possible.

Dedication

To the triple goddess of Mother, Lover and Daughter...

To my Mother, Helen, launcher of a thousand ships. You (and Dad) brought me up to believe in Fun, Tolerance and Understanding. For this I thank you, and will love you both always.

To my Lover, Denise, the wild ecstasy of Dionysus. In you I have the perfect mate with which to practice a life of Joy, Pleasure and Wild Parties. May our love live forever, and if it doesn't, the memory of it will...

To my Daughter, Claire, the fair one. Born on the 23rd of the 5th, you are both a gift and a test, sent by Eris herself, my own Golden Apple. One day you will be old enough to read this book, I hope you do. I hope to pass on to you the spirit of fun my family taught me, and which I practise in my own life. Whatever path you take in life, remember to enjoy it!

My identity is bewilderingly cloudy. I seem to have suffered a great shock - perhaps from some utterly monstrous outgrowth of my cycles of unique, incredible experience. These cycles of experience, of course, all stem from that worm-riddled book.

It was a key - a guide - to certain gateways and transitions of which mystics have dreamed and whispered since the race was young, and which lead to freedoms and discoveries beyond the three dimensions and realms of life and matter that we know.

H. P. Lovecraft

Contents

Foreword

I first became aware of Anton Channing through his writings in Pagan Teenage Voice, a magazine for teenagers provided by Minor Arcana. He was writing under the name Frater M at the time. I had no idea who he could be, but was impressed with the originality of his ideas in Liber Minor, his series of articles about Chaos Magic.

After a brief meeting at a Pagan Conference where we were never actually introduced, we began to correspond about magical theory. It was during this correspondence that I had a more extensive look at the scope of Anton's originality and creativity, as well as his magical genius and perhaps most importantly, his sense of fun and how it relates to his magic. As the association grew closer, I was privileged to be allowed to read the thus far finished chapters of a major project he was working on, the Kaos Hieroglyphica.

The importance of this work was immediately apparent. Building on the symbolism and experiments of both the old Alchemists as well as relatively new magical writers like Peter J Carroll, Anton had created a complete system of magic which was unique, and yet familiar in many of its components. He had actually improved on the previous systems, adding new elements from the perspective of modern usage and his own well educated background and technical expertise in modern cyber culture.

The Cybermorphic Kaosphere System was already gaining widespread popularity through the Internet. Magicians from many paths were able to apply it to their own ideas of magic on a global scale, and yet the book expands much further than the original article which explains the system itself. Anton's own philosophies of magic and of life are influenced by many great philosophers such as John Dee, Idries Shah, Timothy Leary, Austin Osman Spare, Robert Anton Wilson, Sun Tzu, Aleister

Crowley and Kahil Gibran, yet there is always that extra reach beyond the ideas of others in the works of Anton Channing. His originality and unique perspective of life always manages to surpass the ideas of his various influences and to see those things which seem so obvious once they are written on paper or voiced in conversation, and yet do not occur to the average person. His observation of time as a resource, every bit as important as money, is one example of this awakened perspective.

I have had the pleasure of watching him create the drawings which are found throughout the book, and to share his insightful subtleties of symbolism which permeate this artwork which is so much more than decorative. His ability to express ideas in pictures is simply amazing. I have seen him express the entire Cybermorphic Kaosphere System over a pint while drawing the diagram on a beer mat for later use, as the entire system could be contained in that single illustration. It is as though he has invented a new Caballah for the Cyber Age, one which speaks to the modern magician and yet holds the constructs of all of the ancient magics within its core.

The colour symbolism which is covered in a large portion of the book also draws on tradition as well as modern ideas, and again, is taken that step further which typifies the writings of Anton Channing. While acknowledging that colours can be an individual matter of preference, Anton has given us a system which makes sense in a way that transcends nitpicking about personal variation or tradition, but rather gives us a colour symbolism which covers all of the aspects of an intact system which works.

As if that weren't enough for one volume, Anton has also taken us on a journey through history to discover precedents for the symbol of the eight-rayed star, which is so prevalent among modern Chaos Magicians who have largely adopted it from Warhammer games and the novels of Michael Moorcock. His own symbol of the Kaos Hieroglyph draws on this history as well as Alchemical symbology to create a new symbol for a new magic, one which draws on the best elements of all that has gone before.

Among the other special moments I have had in sharing Anton's discoveries during the finishing of this book, has been his own childlike wonder at the degree to which various systems of divination seemed to just fall into place in relating to each other and to his own versions of them. The interrelation of magical ideas plays a major role in this work, and it is very much to Anton's credit that he has allowed these associations to reveal themselves to him at their own pace rather than trying to force them into a prescribed pattern as so many occult writers have done in the past.

Anton Channing's intellectual style of writing expresses the intertwining of these ideas as well as his inspired additions in a pertinent manner which may require more than one reading by the average reader, as there is so much to glean from the subtleties of expression within these pages. His sense of fun, so well known as a component of his previous articles, may play a more recondite role amidst the seriousness of this work, but it clearly winks at us from time to time as we make our journey of discovery through the pages of this illustrious tome of the Great Work, the Kaos Heiroglyphica.

0. Introduction

How to do magic

Under the right conditions, a thought or visualisation of some phenomenon can create an etheric pattern which couples with that phenomenon to modify its behaviour. Conversely, the ether from some phenomenon can couple with a mental image of that phenomenon and modify it to provide divinatory information.

Peter J. Carroll

This book will never explicitly tell you 'how to do magic', indeed this book is not even primarily concerned with magic. None the less, a secondary aim of this book is to entice the novice into discovering their own magical self, and their own natural aptitude for magic. It also aims at awakening new magical inspiration and discovery in the experienced magician. The reason there are no explicit instructions, beyond suggestions for symbolism and a few sample rituals[1], is that all magicians have their own unique magic within, which they must discover for themselves if they are to attain any magical success. So let this book inspire in you your own methods of magic, for only these will be of use to you.

The primary concern of this book is alchemy, by which is meant personal and cultural transformation. Through the process of alchemy, we learn how to transform our base selves into self-empowered individuals, capable of achieving our wildest dreams, be they magical, mystical or more mundane. Some take longer than others on this path of the great work, but despair not, for the journey itself can be an exciting and enjoyable adventure, if you let it.

Although this work draws heavily on traditional alchemical

---

[1] *which must not be mistaken for instruction*

16

symbolism, it is by no means meant to represent an accurate portrayal of medieval alchemy. In fact this books aims to present a new alchemy, an alchemy fit for the New Aeon, the age of Grummet, the Chaoist Aeon or the Aeon of Maat. There is no longer a need for alchemy to attempt transformation dictated by the monotheist ideals of the sixteenth century Hermetic, or even the atheist restrictions of systems such as Jung's. With this book as your guide, you may traverse your vast sea of possible selves, becoming the 'self', you always wanted to be. There is no longer any need for a concept of a 'True Self', for the only truth is the ever changing truth of beauty, and beauty is where you make it. If you feel transformed as a result of reading this book then it will have achieved the purpose on which it embarked when you first opened its pages. You have been warned...

What is Chaos?

The truth is "Mess" is not Khaos. It's the final fruits of Order, it's ultimate manifestation, pattern within pattern, until it all goes wrong. Nobody plans or designs a junkyard... they plan perfect pieces of machinery. Yet everyone knows a junkyard's where they'll end up. But there is no waste in nature. Khaos is a continually creating and destroying system, always fluid, always dynamic, and never wasting a drop.

Deadlock[2]

Chaos Magic is true Natural Magic. There is a strong current of natural themes in modern magical systems, reflecting worldwide concern of humankind's impact on our environment. However, many mistakenly look to nature for a new order, a new dogma, a new truth, and a new ultimate reality. The original Wiccan freedom cry of 'An it harm none, do what thou will', has been perverted by many into a new straightjacket of unbreakable

---

2 Pat Mills and Tony Skinner, *'Khronicles of Khaos'* (London, 1997)

law. That nature itself is neither disordered, nor ordered may seem a shocking concept to those dualistic individuals who cannot conceive of a third possibility, but magicians, mystics and alchemists throughout time and space have always known this simple truth. Now even scientists are beginning to catch up and learn these secrets.

The rhythms and patterns of nature, like the rhythms and patterns of life, are naturally chaotic. Our hearts beat an irregular pattern, the circuits governing its beat are fractal. Should it ever beat in a precisely ordered rhythm, then it is a sign of impending heart attack. Chaos is everything living. Order is everything decaying. Disorder is everything dead. Chaos reproduces itself in patterns of infinite variations. Order tries to keep reproducing itself the same over and over, but ultimately becomes useless as a result of its inability to keep up with change. Order then produces Disorder. To Chaos, Order and Disorder are but toys in its Great Cosmic Play.

But this description is itself flawed. For what of that other meaning of Chaos? That great unknowable source of our existence, Chaos Unmanifest. Is this alive? Surely terms such as 'alive' or 'dead' are meaningless to that place. Well, probably, but then so might be the concept of meaninglessness, so all we can do is speculate. And this is what humankind has done for millennia. Sometimes it dresses up Chaos Unmanifest as an old man with a big white beard whose every wish comes true (as in Christian mythology), at others it portrays it as a random nothingness from which all of existence sprang forth by accident (as in Atheist mythology). Either speculation looks equally ridiculous when you look at them. One might be tempted to create our own stories and ideas, and perhaps it is well we should, but I shall say no more.

This book is not directly a book of Chaos, but a book of alchemical transformation. In these pages you will learn the arts of recognising and transforming the various aspects of yourself, and therefore ultimately your whole self from the base lead into the pure gold (and vice versa, depending on your intent). But since Chaoist ideas also heavily influence this work you will also learn how to reach beyond the gold (or beyond lead, if that be your preferred direction).

Right Hand Path and Left Hand Path

White Magic leans more toward the
acquisition of wisdom and a general feeling of faith
in the universe. The Black form is concerned
more with the acquisition of power and is
reflective of a basic faith in oneself. The end
results are likely to be not dissimilar, for the paths
meet in a way impossible to describe.

Initiates are at liberty to work with material
from either or both. The so-called middle way, or
path of knowledge, consisting of the acquisition of
second-hand ideas, is an excuse to do neither and
leads nowhere.

Peter J. Carroll[3]

These terms are archaic and would seem to have little
relevance to any holistic magical system, a system that aimed at
the liberation of all aspects of the self, be they light or dark.
However, there still seem to be a large number of individuals who
proclaim themselves one or other of these two titles and then
proceed to show prejudice and ignorance concerning people who
call themselves the opposite. Similar problems occur from the
phrases 'Black Magician' and 'White Magician', 'White Witch'
and 'Black Witch', although these terms tend to be used by the
naive beginner[4], or the non-magician.

I have felt it necessary to include a brief discussion of this
issue in the introduction to this book because the terms 'Left
Hand Path' and 'Right Hand Path' are still being used in a
dualistic and prejudicial manner by experienced magicians who
should know better. It should be possible for each magician to
practise their chosen path to illumination without making the

---

3 Peter J Carroll, *'Liber Null & Psychonaut'*, (York Beach,
Maine, 1987), p. 25.
4 *Or the experienced magician having a bit of fun...*

unnecessary assumption that the other path is inferior. The two paths do meet, after all is it really possible to have faith in the universe without faith in oneself, or faith in oneself without faith in the universe? Is it not wise to acquire power, and powerful to acquire wisdom?

So let us leave behind the petty tribalisms that have only ever lead to conflict in all of human history. The path of power and the path of wisdom are both equally useful routes to magical illumination and neither should be rejected out of hand. Some magicians will find it easier to practise one or the other, some will find it easier to do both. It must always be remembered that whether you have decided to acquire wisdom or power first is simply a matter of your own personal taste, and just because you feel more at home with your choice, it does not mean that those who choose differently are in any way inferior, or that they are 'evil', 'bad' or 'dangerous'. I have met dangerous individuals on either path. The danger comes as a result of personal imbalance, and not as a result of the individual's allegiance.

If you are a relatively well balanced individual, then it is probably safer to adopt a self-centred path, a left hand path approach, as the main danger to your balance will come from trying to have faith in a map of the universe which is itself not in balance. If you can put the faith in yourself, recognise that you are yourself well balanced, then you will be able to correct any imbalance in the cosmic map you use. A cosmic map is a complete metaphysical description of the universe. Like maps of physical terrain, they are guides only, abstractions of reality designed to help make navigation easier. A bad map can lead to all sorts of trouble. Examples of cosmic maps include the Qabala, the Runes, the Bible, the Pentagram and this book. Some of these are more distorted than others. Make your choices wisely.

The main danger of left-hand path magic lies in the realm of being unbalanced in yourself. Unless you recognise any imbalances that you possess, and deliberately work at correcting them, then you are in serious danger of using magic to push the imbalance in the wrong direction, giving yourself a mental breakdown.

If you are brave enough to admit that you are currently

slightly imbalanced, or you feel that your personal temperament is just not suited to the path of power, then it is probably better to adopt a right hand path strategy. When dealing with forces as potentially dangerous as magic, it is only wise to make sure that you are in a fit mental state, otherwise you are liable to destroy yourself. The main danger inherent in placing faith in the universe, rather than the self, is that you may inadvertently choose a map of the universe that is in itself out of balance. There are many current magical systems that are out of balance, either because they are hierarchical in their mapping of the universe, or because they are based entirely on the worship of one deity. Both patriarchal 'God' systems and matriarchal 'Goddess' systems tend to exhibit such an imbalance, as do any systems that work exclusively with the light, or exclusively with the dark for that matter. Systems that place the 'ether' as being more important than the four elements are no more or less imbalanced than systems that do the opposite. Qabala can be a good system of magic provided that you don't fall into the trap of assuming one part of the tree is more important than any other. Some systems place more importance on right brain functions, whilst others place more importance on the left brain. Either bias can result in an unbalanced system. A particularly common mistake is to serve a system based entirely on one planetary energy. Solar and Lunar based cults are the main culprits for making this kind of mistake.

If you are of a particularly unbalanced state of mind, it is recommended that you attempt no magic of any kind at all until you can correct this. If you must do anything, then stick to the gentle stillness of meditation and find help before attempting any magic that may seriously escalate your decline. It is likely that any perceived problems that you attempt to correct will exist only in your own mind. Any attempt to correct these illusory problems will usually remove you even further from correcting the real problem and will only make your situation worse. Study as much of the various cosmological and magickal maps of the universe as possible. Try and identify where your own weaknesses lie, but make no attempt to correct them straight away. By expanding your knowledge of cosmological systems, and your own weaknesses, you will be working to correct them automatically. Healing yourself in this manner can take time. Be patient and you will reap a good harvest.

Some individuals who find themselves having an interest in magic will have even worse problems, self-destructive sub-personalities, known to experienced magicians as demons. Demons will do everything in their power to prevent the individual progressing to a state of mind capable of dealing with them. They can be very powerful, and it is not recommended that an aspiring inexperienced magician tries to deal with their demons alone, or without sound advice. If you do, you may well succeed, but why take the risk when you can get help from an experienced demonologist? However, when seeking help from others in the magical community, it is well to remember that there are many self-proclaimed magicians who are incapable of dealing with this situation. Be cautious of anyone whose reaction to your problem is melodramatic, especially if they start talking about psychic vampires or magical attack. Use your own judgement to determine the experience and competence of anyone you think might be able to help.

The purpose of this book is to put forward a non-hierarchical, non-biased cosmological system that draws on the alchemical influences behind Carroll's 'Eight Colours'. It is hoped that the system is complete and workable in itself, and that it contains no innate imbalance. However, I don't advise that you take my word for it. Also, it is entirely possible that you find meanings in my words that are other than the meanings I intended, which lead you to an imbalanced perception of my system. It is recommended that any magician gains at least basic familiarity with as many systems as possible. In this way any real or perceived imbalances may be corrected.

1. The Cybermorphic Kaosphere System

He handles the planets and weights their dust,
he mounts on the comet's car,
And he lifts the veil of the sun, and stares in the
eyes of the uttermost star...
Alfred Austin[5]

Chaos Magicians and other sorcerors have used the eight coloured chaosphere system of magick as presented by Pete Carroll in Liber Kaos to a fair amount of success. Perhaps it is this success which has caused few, if any, magicians to openly question what other inner secrets it may reveal. Perhaps those magicians interested in the more abstract mysticism of studying a system in depth have turned to studying Kabala on the side. Perhaps those of us that used it have been content to just treat the chaosphere as a simple way of describing and giving a category to different types of magic. For what ever reason, the innate depth and mysticism of the system seems to have been overlooked.

The first thing one might notice about the chaosphere is that it is made up four axis. It is very surprising that no-one has openly attempted to attribute traditional elemental correspondences to these axis. One explanation is the awkward problems and inconsistencies that such an exercise unravels. We have preferred to work in ignorance of the limitations of this magical system rather than correct these inconsistencies. Not that I am intending to criticise them for this, for despite the inaccuracies they have still managed not only some very powerful and effective magic. No, criticism is not the reason for my drawing attention to these errors, my reason is that a considered correction of them can lead to a better understanding of our magical system and hence the continued survival of a refreshed and enlivened magical tradition fit for the fifth aeon.

I now present my thoughts, starting with an elemental analysis

---

5 Michael Moorcock, *'The End of All Songs'*, p. 295.

24

and showing all workings out and arguments. The first problem I found myself confronted with when trying to work out elemental correspondences is where to begin. The names and colours are more a distraction than a guide. I decided to look at the natures of the polarities. I found that there seemed to be two pairs of polarities, the + (cross) and the x (ex). The + seemed to be object-oriented, whereas x seemed to be process-oriented. I decided to name these 'being' and 'doing' respectively. I then analysed the + pair of axis, the 'being' pair. It struck me within this pairing that the vertical, yellow-octarine pair seemed to be about the self being/object, and further to this a vertical line is the letter I. Contrastingly the horizontal, orange-blue axis would seem to be about how one relates to other beings/objects[6]. I thus created a sub-polarity within the + pair. I decided to name the sub-polarity the self/other sub-polarity.

Next I analysed the x pair of axis, the doing pair. On a closer inspection it would seem that the sex/death axis relates to dividing processes, whilst the love/war axis appears to be about uniting processes. Sex, or creation, is about the separation of a new complex being/object from the self. This may be the result of a loving union but at the end of the day sex is about separation. Death is about the decay process, or entropy, where all the constituent parts of an object are separated and spread about evenly by stochastic mechanisms. Love is about mutual union, a combining of two forces, on equal or fair terms, in order to form a third new thing. Contrastingly, war is a forced union, where one thing takes another thing over and makes it a part of itself. Although in effect a new third thing is created, it allows the illusion of the "winner" continuing as itself after having consumed the loser. This connection between War and Consumption suggests that the connection between conflict and hunting, and the fact that

---

[6] *This might not be immediately apparent from the colours and names of the magics, but I have chosen to present the reasoning for this later on in this chapter, since it detracts from the simplicity of the current calculations.*

Mars was originally a god of agriculture, are more than just coincidences.

At this stage I found it useful to tabulate my observations to make it easier to analyse them. As you can see from the table below, the results are not without their problems. However, the problems seem to be more in Pete Carroll's structuring of the system rather than with my own observations. I realise that is a bold statement to make and I will attempt to argue my case.

Axis	Dualities	Positive polarity	Negative polarity
Identity (Fire)	Being: Self	Ego (Yellow)	Magick (Octarine)
Resources (Earth)	Being: Other	Thinking (Orange)	Wealth (Blue)
Separation (Air)	Doing: Divide	Sex (Purple)	Death (Black)
Attraction (Water)	Doing: Unite	Love (Green)	War (Red)

I am not the first one to have noticed an odd inconsistency with the thinking-wealth "polarity". Sex/Death and Love/War are easy to spot polarities. The Ego/Magick polarity takes a little thought[7] but is feasible. Thinking/Wealth just doesn't make sense

---

[7] *It may be feasible, but I have decided that the fact that it takes a little thought is a sign that this polarity also needs some attention. It is interesting to note that all the problems in the chaosphere are on the +, the being polarity. The reason this is interesting is that Pete Carroll's writings betray an extreme bias against object-oriented thinking, to such an extent that he seemed to wish to eradicate all concept of being from the way we think. Perhaps it is time to address this serious imbalance at*

as a polarity. The other main problem is with octarine or pure magic. The correct elemental correspondence for octarine magick would be Ether, the life force energy that Austin Osman Spare named 'Kia'. This would suggest that Octarine should never have been one of the eight colours, but should be drawn at the centre of the chaosphere, with the four elemental axis emanating from it.

To replace Octarine at the top of the chaosphere I propose Psyche magick. White, Aquamarine or Pearl are the suggested colours. My reasoning for this is that it is the negative polarity of the identity axis, reflecting the inner self. Mysticism is the study of the inner workings of thyself, the psyche. In this sense, psychology is essentially atheist mysticism. Ego magic remains unchanged as the outward expression of the self. I also suggest a vague association to the planetary energy of Neptune, which H. T. Cannibal describes, in her paper "Symbolism of the planets"...

> Neptune shows the need to escape from physical and material limitations and find spiritual wholeness, our impressionability, evasiveness, compassion and idealism, illusion and fantasy.

This, in addition to the renaming of Thinking and Wealth magick as Work and Play magic causes the table to look quite different...

Axis	Dualities	Positive polarity	Negative polarity
Identity (Fire)	Being: Self	Ego (Yellow)	Psyche (White)
Resources (Earth)	Being: Other	Work (Orange)	Play (Blue)
Separation (Air)	Doing: Divide	Sex (Purple)	Death (Black)

the heart of Chaos Magic.

Attraction (Water)	Doing: Unite	Love (Green)	War (Red)

You may be wondering why I have chosen the new names Work and Play for orange and blue magick. Pete Carroll's ideas about wealth seemed nice in theory but seemed to contradict my own observations[8] that if you really wanted serious money, you'd have to work for it. Blue magic only seemed to succeed in getting one off handouts of cash and/or time for spending/using when there was something you wanted to spend it on. I propose that this is because blue magic is about spending or using resources, whilst earning it is more related to the stress and activity of orange magic and mercury. Thus I came to draw the following table. The old name of the magic is in the parentheses.

Orange - **Work Magick** (Thinking Magick)	Blue - **Play Magick** (Wealth Magick)
Mercury	Jupiter
Servant, Submissive	Master, Dominant
Work, Effort, Business, Stress	Play, Rest, Pleasure, Relaxation
Earning, Accumulating Resources	Using, Spending Resources
Haste	Sloth
Quick	Slow
Excited	Peaceful
Energetic	Calm

---

[8] *I was directed to the inconsistencies by Sor. Syzygy 1239, 2° IOT*

I propose an end to the idea of blue magic being about wealth, it is only a half truth and a distracting half-truth at that! Using a system of negative and positive polarities I suggest both the new name Resource Magic and the correspondence with the entire Orange-Blue axis, rather than just the blue polarity. Incidentally the only way to have play without work is to get other people do the work for you. In British society there are only two ways to do this and they are to be unemployed or to own a successful business.

The drawback of these changes is that Thinking Magic no longer seems to exist. In fact I believe that thinking magic has been more effectively liberated from the unnecessary restrictions placed on it by Carroll's system. There are many types of thinking and they can now all be attributed to various magical categories depending upon the nature of the thinking taking place.

The quick 'thinking without thinking' technique described by Carroll would fit into Work magic in most cases, as would the acquisition of professional skills, logical thought is an operation of separation magick, air magick. Thinking about your own thoughts (self reflection) would fit most comfortably in Psyche magick.

In my new proposed chaosphere system, there are considerably more categories of magic than before, sixteen in all, with a lot more correspondences between them. In addition I propose the following shorthand for the types of magic, based on their expression as either a positive or negative polarity. Also listed is the corresponding symbol from Hermetic Alchemy for those fascinated by magickal correspondences (as I am!).

Magical Type	Colour/Element	Notation	Symbol(s)
Kaos Magic	Kaos Unmanifest	∞	✳ @
Pure Magic	Octarine (Ether, Alchemical Mercury)	o	☿ ⊗ ♉
Being Magic	Soul (Alchemical Salt)	–	⊖
Doing Magic	Spirit (Alchemical Sulphur)	+	♀
Identity Magic	Wand (Fire)	– –	△↑
Resource Magic	Pentacle (Earth)	– +	▽ O
Separation Magic	Sword (Air)	+ –	▲ †
Attraction Magic	Cup (Water)	+ +	▽ ◡
Psyche Magic	White (Neptune)	– – –	♆
Ego Magic	Yellow (Sun)	– – +	☉
Play Magic	Blue (Jupiter)	– + –	♃
Work Magic	Orange (Mercury)	– + +	☿
Death Magic	Black (Saturn)	+ – –	♄
Sex Magic	Purple (Moon)	+ – +	☾
War Magic	Red (Mars)	+ + –	♂
Love Magic	Green (Venus)	+ + +	♀

The intention of this notation is that it helps show up the correspondences, but also it helps to show the binary nature of the system. It perhaps also reveals, less misleadingly, the dualities which need to be transcended in order to do Octarine, or pure magick properly. It is also hoped that this new system has corrected the bias in favour of Doing which Carroll's work had displayed, perhaps itself as a reaction against the bias in favour of Being inherent in most right hand path magic. I'm not sure if the notation will prove widely useful in magic but it presents a simple way of conducting a mystical analysis of the chaosphere system.

As the final part of my analysis, I present the revised table, this time with the proposed binary notation in place. This is followed by some notes on the revised chaosphere system and a corresponding diagram. This proposed new system is intended to expand upon the old chaosphere system without invalidating that system. It is also hoped that it will open up the system to mystical reflection, in the spirit of the newly revealed Psyche Magic. Psyche magic, or mysticism, has been in other systems all along, even Atheism has psychology, it's own brand of mysticism. Until now, Chaos magicians have been forced to draw on the mysticisms of other systems. Of course, this is itself just another system that magicians can take or not as they please.

Pure Octarine (o)			
Axis	Dualities	Positive polarity	Negative polarity
Identity (Fire)	Being(-): Self(--)	Ego Yellow (--+)	Psyche White (---)
Resources (Earth)	Being(-): Other(-+)	Work Orange (-++)	Play Blue (-+-)
Separation (Air)	Doing(+): Divide(+-)	Sex Purple (+-+)	Death Black (+--)
Attraction (Water)	Doing(+): Unite(++)	Love Green (+++)	War Red (++-)

The New Cybermorphic Kaosphere System

Information technologists conventionally recognise two classes of information - Data and Instructions. I would like to add a third class: Systems structure control information; lets designate information packages conforming to this description as 'Cyber-morphs'.

The principle difference between a cyber-morph and data/instruction information is that while data and instructions always relate directly to some physical reality, cyber-morphs relate essentially to the abstract systems framework within which those data and instructions have meaning and/or validity.

Charles Brewster[9]

Charles Brewster, in his book Liber Cyber, presents us with the concept of cybermorphic information, as quoted above. Brewster then uses the example of magic squares, where numbers are arranged in a square grid such that every row, column and diagonal add up to the same total. In this example the set of natural numbers are the data, the rules for arranging the numbers in the grid are the instructions and the strange property of the square to have all the rows add up to the same number is the cyber-morph.

To make a distinction between the old chaosphere and the new one I am presenting, I have adopted the convention of spelling the word with a 'K', instead of a 'Ch', when talking about the new system. The chaosphere did not exhibit cybermorphic properties in that it did not seem to provide any information other than the data and instructions. That is not to say that the cyber-morph wasn't there, just that it takes work such as the work I have performed to reach the Kaosphere model, to reveal it.

On a metaphysical level, it can be said that Data corresponds

---

[9] Charles Brewster, *Liber Cyber* (UK, 1991)

to Being/Objects/Soul whilst Instructions correspond to Doing/Processes/Spirit. Cyber-morph information corresponds to Kia/Ether/Octarine, which is the mysterious life force energy[10] that represents the boundary between the Kaos Unmanifest and what we experience as existence.

At the centre of the Kaosphere is the Kaos Unmanifest, everything and nothing merged together in a strange non-existence of infinite possibilities. At the very edge of that Kaos is the Kia energy of the universe, the level of Pure Octarine Life force, the Ether. The macro-Kia contains all of our personal Kia. This is the cybermorphic level of magic where the infinite possibilities in the non-existent Kaos fight to become part of existence and where existence fights to influence the possibilities of non-existent manifesting Kaos. It is like the boundary between the set of complex numbers included in the Mandlebrot set and those that aren't, impossible to determine a definite edge between the two, but easy to see approximately where that infinite edge lies. For a given point it is easy to determine whether it is part of existence or the non-existent primal Kaos, but to be able to accurately define the boundary between the two would take an infinitely detailed map. Magic takes place in the region where reality and fantasy meet.

This etheric octarine force divides into duality or existence. The first duality to appear in existence is the being/doing duality. Science has recently discovered this duality in the form of the debate concerning particles (beings) or waves (doings). Computer programming is also aware of the distinction between objects and processes. In truth the universe is not made up of beings or

---

[10] *The words 'energy' and 'force' are both quite misleading when discussing the Kia or Ether, and have lead to many New-Age over simplifications, so I will try to avoid using them when describing this level of reality. The reader is urged to interpret any such descriptions, in this book or any other, as being colourful metaphor. Understand and be aware that the terms are used with 'poetic licence'...*

doings, both are just as illusionary. That is not to say that neither are there, just that the observation of either is at the expense of recognising that human experience doesn't really take place on that level and magic can take place on either. Magic in its purest form takes us to the Octarine level, and possibly even into the Kaos beyond if we are lucky. However, it is impossible to do all the work a magician needs to perform whilst working purely with Octarine magic. Therefore it is sometimes essential to recognise the existence of a particular being or a particular doing. Indeed, it is often necessary to reach deeper into duality and closer to everyday perception even than these.

'Being magic', or Soul magic, inevitably divides into magic on your own souls, or on other beings' souls. Then there is your inner self (Psyche) and your outward self (Ego). Other souls can be used for your own personal pleasure (Play), but first you need to collect or organise them into a state where this is possible (Work).

'Doing magic', or Spirit magic, concerns movement and change. At the extremes of this, there is movement which involves the coming together of two doings, and movement which involves their separation. Sometimes two doings come together and combine to form a new third doing (Love). At other times one of the doings consumes the other doing so that only one remains (War). Sometimes a separation involves a doing appearing to emit a second extra doing whilst remaining intact itself (Sex). At other times a doing appears to separate into two or more unrecognisable doings, neither resembling the previous doing[11] (Death).

---

[11]*Although the associated being may not have changed much. If you think about it in this way it can be seen that the spirit of someone departs on death, but the soul may linger. Cremation should help speed the souls departure. It could be interesting to study how many ghosts are of buried corpses to discover if they are 'lost souls' or 'spirit imprints'. They may be neither but this is an area for those interested to study. As in most subjects in life, I expect the reality is somewhat a mixture of all theories...*

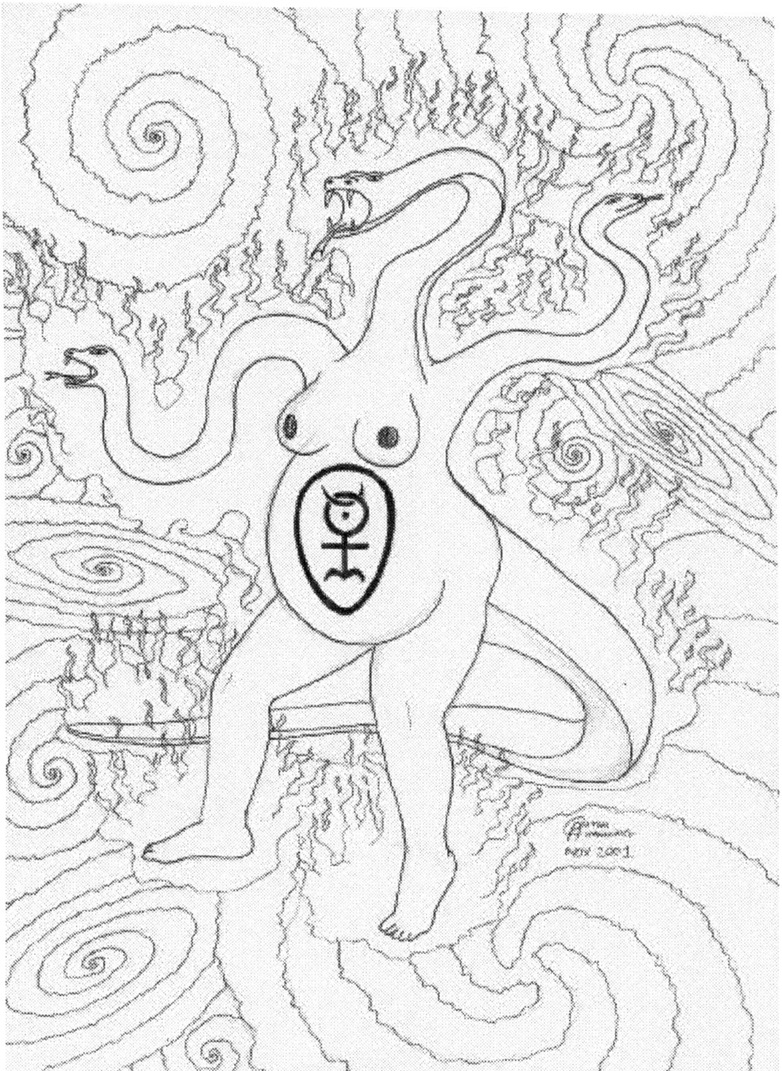

2. Pure Magick

Total freedom, responsibility and interspecies
harmony will make the voyage possible.
You must transcend larval identities
of race, culture and nationality.
Your only allegiance is to life.
Dr. Timothy Leary

Pure Magick, (Octarine Magick) in the Kaosphere system
has been relocated to the centre, to represent that it is
transcendent of duality and existence. It is even transcendent of
the resulting paradoxical duality between duality (existence) and
non-duality (non-existence). It is no longer introvert in nature, but
neither is it extrovert. Its place as introverted magic has been
taken over by psyche magick, or white magick. Pure Magick is
now transcendent of that duality and can be considered ambivert,
if anything at all.

All magick essentially makes use of Octarine Magick, indeed
no magick can take place without it. Gnosis is the state of mind
that a magician must reach for successful magic to take place. All
gnosis is essentially transcendent of duality at the moment it
works, even if the pathway to gnosis itself is firmly rooted in
duality. This is simply because magick needs to manipulate the
Kia in order to work in any way other than psychologically.
Psychological magic can itself be very powerful, but is
materialistic in its nature, and hence limited to working within a
materialist framework. Since this framework is not always
sufficient for the successful outcome of all spells, it is
recommended that a serious magician learn to work successfully
on the Octarine level. The psychological level is also very useful,
and the most effective rituals will be designed to work on both
levels.

For this chapter we will concentrate on how to work
successful Octarine magic, how to manipulate the cybermorphic
ether, how to use your Kia. A good starting point for this
examination is the original chapter on Octarine Magic in Liber
Kaos by Carroll. However, an examination of this chapter reveals

very little concerning the nature of Octarine Magic. The chapter is half anecdotal and one third concerned with what we should now call Psyche Magick.

Auric Magick

I suggest that Carroll's chapter on Auric Magic[12] is of more relevance, although Auric Magic is only one way of manipulating the Kia. I have decided that a slightly modified quote from this chapter should explain exactly what auric magick is, and why it is most properly considered an Octarine application, even when used in other magickal spheres. The word cybermorphic, in bold has been added by myself, and is really only there to describe the kind of information that is exchanged, and otherwise leaves Carroll's meaning unchanged.

> [Auric Magick] ...works by an exchange of **cybermorphic** information (not energy) between the subconscious (not the body) and its environment, which can include the body. Projected **cybermorphic** information can select the immediate future of a situation and creates what appears to be an occult effect. Similarly, received **cybermorphic** information can be perceived as a bodily sensation even though it is not received by the body directly.

As we have already seen, cybermorphic information properly corresponds to the Octarine level. Magickal energy, Kia or Ether are considered to actually be cybermorphic information. I would argue that the subconscious is not the only level the exchange of information can take place from, and that in my experience non-physical entities have proved quite adept at using auric magick for their purposes. In all, I would define Auric Magic as a function of Octarine magick in which cybermorphic information is passed

---

[12] Peter J Carroll, *'Liber Kaos'*, (York Beach, ME, 1992), pp. 101-05

directly between an entity and its environment, allowing direct manipulation of the cybermorphic level of reality without recourse to spells and/or ritual.

This kind of Octarine Magic is mostly used in response to urgent need. For example I once found myself in a situation where someone I shared a house with was threatening me. I had offended them by making a meal for someone who he apparently considered to be his ex-girlfriend. His behaviour was obviously irrational but I nonetheless found myself outside in the street with this guy, who was preparing to hit me. This is an ideal situation in which to perform some impromptu Auric Magic, although a far from ideal situation in which to find oneself. I projected the information for a protective aura into the space around me, which included sending information about this directly into my would be opponents mind. The idea was that they should not be able to punch through the protection. However, the protection did not exist as some kind of force-field, it only worked because I managed to send a packet of cybermorphic information directly into my aggressor's mind, causing them to subconsciously believe that they could not hit me. As a result, their punch appeared to deflect about 90° and into a brick wall, causing them to hurt their fist. So hurt, they lost interest in fighting me.

As with spells, it is necessary to reinforce the intent with actions likely to make a favourable outcome more likely. In the case above, whilst anticipating attack and readying myself for a quick counter attack if necessary, I stood in a non-aggressive position with my hands at my sides. I used a face that smiled in smug amusement, as if I knew something about the situation my opponent didn't. My opponent was also aware that I had trained in Tae Kwon Do and was the proud owner of a 1st Dan black-belt. All this added up to a situation where it was highly likely that my opponent had become doubtful of his desire to fight me. Obviously I never revealed to him the magick I had used, as it would have been counter-productive to do so at the time, and I no longer know the individual concerned.

Several months later I was in the living room with all my housemates, the same individual now aware that I am a magician. We were all preparing to sit down and watch a video. The video player had been playing up, often badly damaging the tapes. It was playing up on this particular night and suddenly I found myself the centre of attention. Everyone looked at me as my housemate said that as I was a magician, why couldn't I do some magic to get it working. So I sat cross-legged on the floor and meditated, and in that state of complete balance and calm I sent cybermorphic information to the video player, instructing it to work. After about five minutes of meditation I sat up and told them it was ready. I had not touched the video or the video player and no-one else had fiddled with it whilst I was meditating. To everyone's amazement the video did actually work and we were able to watch it from beginning to end with out anything going wrong.

In this way, I had sent a packet of information to the video, delaying its inevitable failure long enough for us to watch a film. I had no particular desire to fix the video player permanently, as I have no wish to become a psychic repair-man, besides which a permanent fix would almost certainly have taken more effort than I was prepared to expend.

There is nothing spectacular to the magician about the above examples I have given. If you ever get the chance to talk to an experienced magician then they will be able to give you plenty more of such anecdotes, should you require them. It should be noted that the description of Auric Magic given here is intended to be an alternative and liberating paradigm for the working of Auric Magick to previous descriptions given by Carroll and especially the overly dogmatic systems found in much of the popular books on the subject. The individual magician should be encouraged to use whatever belief and/or system works best for them, usually this will mean adapting and combining existing systems found elsewhere and based on the magicians own experiences/observations.

If you find it easy using a system which unnecessarily limits what you can do with it, and are having problems believing in a system that would address those limitations, then it is probably time to undergo a major working of paradigm shifting and random belief. Such an exercise should be more than enough to limber up those lax belief muscles to make breaking the chains of your existing beliefs an easier task.

Any discussion of Auric Magick would be incomplete without an investigation of what an aura might be. For the purposes of this argument, the Author has chosen to discuss what an aura might be in a binary information system model of reality, as suggested by Ramsey Dukes in many of his books, by the films 'The Matrix' and 'Total Recall', an old episode of 'Red Dwarf' and even by some models of Quantum Physics. According to this theory, the universe as we know it is actually 'simulated' on something we would call a computer, but probably wouldn't recognise as such since it exists outside of our universe.

We are either beings from the outside universe that have connected into this reality, like we might play a computer game or visit a virtual reality simulation, or we are actually artificial intelligences within the system. This is not as far-fetched as it sounds. As I write I am using a home PC whose processing power is roughly equivalent to the brain of an ant. Current home PCs have a processing power equivalent to the brain of a fly. The last predictions I saw suggested that the processing power of new PC computers in the year 2010 would have a processing speed equivalent to a human mind! Artificial Intelligence technology has been held up largely due to insufficient processing power. Once computers can match the human mind in terms of complexity, it will only be a matter of time before we are able to create simulated humans. By the year 2050 an average home computer may be so powerful we will be able to run a whole world each.

To be able to model a complex three dimensional reality we would need to be continuously detecting for collisions, or what we would call physical contact. A human being is an amazingly complex three-dimensional structure, and the mathematics involved in detecting a collision would be very complex and processor hungry. It would only make sense to simplify the calculations somewhat. A relatively easy shape to detect collisions for would be a sphere. All one would have to do in order to determine whether any point of an object collided with the sphere, would be to measure the distance of the point from the centre of the sphere. If this distance is less than the radius of sphere then the objects have collided. In the case of a human aura, any object entering the aura is not automatically in collision with the body, but any object that has not entered the aura can be immediately excluded from the calculations. Since the majority of objects in the universe will be outside of a human aura at any one time, this drastically reduces the number of complex calculations that need to take place.

In this model the planet Earth would also have an aura, which would represent the boundary of its immediate influence. All small objects inside the Earth's aura would be modelled as part of the Earth object, just as the Earth itself would be modelled as a part of the Solar system object. Each cell of the human body would also be individual objects, considered as part of the human object. The cells would be made up of molecular objects, made up of atomic objects, made up of sub-atomic objects until eventually everything would be described as pure cybermorphic information. In this way the system would be able to drastically reduce the processing for collision detection. A human as part of planet Earth would not only just need to detect for collisions with its own aura, it would only need to detect aura overlap for objects inside the Earth's aura.

If humans are artificial intelligences (at least as far as the outside universe is concerned), then it would make sense to model all the functions (spirits) of an individual human as one object instance (soul) of the class human. Humans that have become self aware of their own binary information (Life force, ether, Kia) can begin to learn how to tamper with the code. We can evolve functions on a level of reality that most life forms, indeed most people, are not aware exists. It would seem that we have to evolve them individually at this point, in that we cannot pass the information for these abilities on to our genetic offspring. We can, however, pass it on memetically to our spiritual associates. Through experimentation we can begin to learn how to 'see' auras, or become aware of them, and learn how to manipulate our own by sending instructions to it. We can easily contact any objects and bodies within our aura, as the aura function of our self-object will automatically be tracking such objects and maintaining an information link with them. As there is already an information channel open between the two objects, it should be a small task to

41

reprogram your aura function to send all sorts of different information to other objects. In this way it could be possible to develop psycho-kenesis, telepathy and other psychic skills on a short range scale.

Having mastered these skills within your own aura, it should then be a small task to reprogram your aura to create for yourself a 'second' aura that you can send great distances for the purpose of long range telepathy, psycho-kenesis and other psychic skills. It may even be entirely possible to de-activate your collision detection so that you can walk through walls! It could even be possible to create an aura that blocks out harmful radiation, generates heat, neutralises heat, even bring whole new objects into existence if you can work out the correct function call. Some of these things may have even started to occur naturally, by a process of natural selection. Increasingly we may begin to notice organisms that have abilities to seemingly alter the very fabric of reality in small ways. The potential for development in this paradigm is intellectually frightening. Indeed, our own fear may be the very thing that blocks our magical development in this area.

Initiation Rituals

"Will you walk into my parlour?" said the Spider to the Fly;
"Tis the prettiest little parlour that ever you did spy;
The way into my parlour is up a winding stair,
And I have many curious things to show when you are there."
"Oh, no, no," said the little Fly, "to ask me is in vain;
For who goes up your winding stair can ne'er come down again."
Mary Howitt[13]

The main purpose of performing an Octarine Magick ritual is to increase, or replenish, your magickal reserves of Kia energy. This is performed by somehow 'tapping into' the flow of Kia in your surroundings and absorbing enough for your needs. This occurs during every ritual, whether or not it is intended to be an Octarine working or not, but in workings of other colours the Kia is immediately used and/or directed into an operation of dualistic intent.

An operation intended to increase ones capacity for manipulating Kia is known as an 'Initiation', and is an entirely special kind of Octarine ritual. Most experienced magicians will be aware that an Initiation working takes months to complete, and that the so-called 'Initiation Ritual' is merely the climatic ending to a long period of work. The actual initiation rituals that a magician puts themselves through will inevitably be more numerous than the levels of initiation offered in various groups and occult schools. Initiatory levels obtained in magickal Orders reflect only the time and commitment (and sometimes other resources) that the magician has put into that Order. It is extremely difficult to ascertain the exact level of a magician, which has little to do with titles earned in any Order, although a powerful magician will be able to quickly recognise another powerful magician and also recognise potential in others. The reason for this is because there is no actual set path for a magician to progress along, although

---

[13] Tony Meeuwissen, *'The Key to the Kingdom'*, (London, 1992), p. 112

43

some schools are more rigid in what they let their magicians study than others. Each magician is free to study areas of magical interest for them, an experienced magician having gained Initiations in many disciplines and occult schools of thought. No two magicians of equal level would have gone through an identical set of Initiations. It stands to reason that two magicians of different levels wouldn't have either, although a very experienced magician may have gone through all the Initiations, and more, of a relatively inexperienced magician. Even in this last example it is unlikely, maybe even impossible, that the two magicians would have experienced all of their shared initiations in exactly the same manner. Even the sequential order the Initiations were gained in will make a difference, as previous experience gained from other Initiations will shape the magicians attitudes towards the current one.

What an Initiation actually is, is hard to define. It is not an objective experience. Two individuals could go through an identical experience, the reading of the same book for example, and one could experience Initiation, and the other just an increase in knowledge. The difference lies in the subjective interpretation of the experience. In this case the initiate would have been able to gain an Illumination from the words of the book, where the second individual merely learned the meaning of the words. The initiate was able to explicitly relate the meanings in the book, to meanings from other books and to meanings attached to other experiences in their own life, to an extent where their view of what constitutes 'reality' becomes challenged, broken and changed. The second individual only manages to see the facts from their own already held point of view. The book doesn't challenge them in any way, or more to the point, the experience of reading the book doesn't challenge them. This may be because they have already advanced beyond the level of the book, finding nothing new in its meanings, or it may be because they have not yet reached a level of understanding capable of interpreting the meanings of the book. More so, it may be because the individual deliberately chooses not to understand.

However, we are more interested in examining the initiate, and what it is that causes an initiation to take place, than we are in why others don't experience initiation. The initiate's beliefs concerning reality are challenged to the extent that they are permanently changed. An experienced magician will have become so used to this happening that they eventually abandon a concrete belief in reality at all. Failure to do this will result in a dogmatic rejection of experiences that do not fit the expectations of belief, and paranoia concerning everyone who appears to be trying to suppress the 'true reality.' An intelligent reader will have no difficulty in realising that if there is a 'true reality' then it is unlikely that it will be themselves that have discovered it. There are millions of intelligent and reasoning people all over the planet, with a variety of political, social and spiritual beliefs. All combinations of beliefs taken in detail will reveal that no two individuals believe exactly the same thing. What chance is there then that the belief structure you have come to hold is the 'true reality' and not just the relative beliefs you have come to hold as a result of your own experiences?

The only intelligent option, when faced with such a dilemma, is to opt for outright agnosticism in its strongest sense. Robert Anton Wilson puts it well when he writes, in block capitals...

I DO NOT BELIEVE ANYTHING.

In agnostic systems of Sorcery, belief becomes a relative tool used in the transformation of consciousness. But why do we transform our consciousness? For what reason does a magician put themselves through such an experience? I hesitate to answer that question, because the ultimate reason will differ from magician to magician, many magicians will only have a vague idea or feeling that drives them, often something that can't be put into words. For myself, I have found that through believing in a magickal paradigm, I have been able increase my potential for pleasure in life and make my life more varied and interesting. I also feel I am now more able to cope with any situation I find myself in without ever being disturbed. The reason consciousness transformation is important for a magician is because it is through the broadening of consciousness and possibilities for belief that the magician increases their capacity for manipulating Kia.

An experienced magician will be continuously undergoing initiation, which literally means that all experiences will be contributing to the magician's magical development. A magician who consciously recognises this will do everything in their power to select experiences that will allow the most desired magical development. Viewed in this way, even the reading of books can be considered an initiatory experience, especially works of fiction. Properly read, many great works of fiction are in themselves a kind of pathworking. For those unfamiliar with the term, a pathworking is a special kind of magical journey that a magician undertakes inside their mind, whilst the physical body is in the stillness of a meditative state. Tony Willis describes pathworkings in his book Discover Runes.

> One might say that Pathworking is a type of meditation which relies for its effects on the use of the imaginative faculty. As opposed to some other forms of meditation technique which advise students to empty their minds, the aim of a Pathworking is to flood consciousness with selected symbolic images. A Pathworking is usually a dramatised story which may be rooted in either history, myth or some other area of fiction.[14]

Often the magician is guided by a voice that leads the pathworking, either a tape recording, or someone else reading it out loud. These journeys are often of an initiatory nature, although they can also be used for other purposes. A good novel can take the reader through a similar experience, especially when the reader is able to identify with one or more of the central characters, or with the ideas presented by the author. My personal preferences in this area have been the works of Michael Moorcock, Leopold von Sacher-Masoch, H. P. Lovecraft, Terry Pratchett, J. R. R. Tolkien, Ursula Le Guin, Roger Zelazny,

---

[14] Tony Willis, *'Discover Runes'*, (London, 1991), p. 166

J.K.Rowling and Philip K. Dick. There are many others, and those that read comics will be able to work out how these can also be used for this purpose.

Of course, if you can actually take the time to devise specific pathworkings based on the stories you have read, then you can enhance their power, or focus it onto a specific area of import within the story. Visualised properly, role-playing games can also be used in a similar way. Be careful what you use though, as some books might alter your mind in ways you wish they hadn't...

Circuit VIII - The neuro-atomic circuit

...contact with alien (extraterrestrial?) "entities" or with a galactic Overmind, etc., such as I've experienced, have all been reported for thousands of years, not merely by the ignorant, the superstitious, the gullible, but often by the finest minds among us (Socrates, Giordano Bruno, Edison, Buckminster Fuller, etc.). Such experiences are reported daily to parapsychologists and have been experienced by such scientists as Dr. John Lilly and Carlos Castaneda.

Robert Anton Wilson

The eighth circuit of Timothy Leary's eight circuit model of the mind appears to be concerned with what Carroll (after Pratchett) has called Octarine magic. There appear to be some problems with the eight circuit model of the mind, mainly caused by an erroneous view of left and right brain functions. The model makes more sense when one reverses any mention of the left and right lobes. The right brain functions are the oldest functions of the brain, the essentially animal brain concerned with reality recognition, pattern recognition and spatial awareness. This strangely seems to agree with Leary's description of the left brain. The left brain is a much more recent evolutionary development. Any special powers that humans will have developed are more likely to lie here, in the lobe concerned with weird abstract thought and abstract logic. The four new functions seem to have more in common with the abstract thoughts of the left brain.

Other than this basic flaw, the other problem is that the model appears to be hierarchical, as a result of the information having been presented in a linear mode. The truth is that the eight circuits are all of equal importance .The human mind has the potential to develop all of these areas. It is possible that some individuals will develop later circuits to a high degree without developing earlier ones, or developing earlier and later ones whilst missing one in the middle, or any combination you can think of. It is most desirable to develop your mind in as balanced a way as possible, as all eight circuits are important to the survival of the self.

I have tried to incorporate the ideas of the eight circuit model into the cybermorphic kaosphere system, in order to show how they might be viewed in a non-linear manner. In Leary's model, the eighth circuit seems to be concerned with a quantum-level awareness, capable of sending information faster than the speed of light. Timothy Leary himself seemed to have an obsession with contacting extra-terrestrial intelligences using telepathy, which could, of course, be one use of this circuit. Circuit VIII also appears to have something to do with time travel and an awareness on this level should be capable of contacting the past, or the future, or even parallel dimensions. Whether we would actually want to do this is another matter. Then again it can be argued, and is argued in Carroll's work, that every enchantment we make selects a preferred parallel future universe for us to exist in. And what is 'Past life recall', if it is not travel into the past, or the forming of some kind of information link with the past.

Robert Anton Wilson and Timothy Leary have both speculated about the many visionaries who see 'extra-terrestrials and/or angels and/or gods', of which there are literally thousands of reports. One speculation is that they are an alien race that have already evolved this ability to such a high degree that they communicate to anyone else in the universe they can find who will listen. They may even be shamans of a primitive alien race that think the humans they contact are actually gods! They could even be humans from the future who are trying to contact us now in the past, or other humans from around the planet who are trying to guide the development of other humans. They may be any combination of any or all of these things, or they may be any number of things that we haven't considered.

Banishing Rituals

"Banishing Rituals" as they are commonly known, serve several purposes. At the beginning and end of longer rituals they serve to establish or re-establish concentration, balance and control. They may also be used for visualisation practise or for shutting out unwanted influences.

Peter J. Carroll[15]

Banishing rituals seem to have an Octarine flavour to them. Performed at the beginning of a ritual they seem to perform the functions of blocking out unwanted influences, establishing focus and concentration and opening a conscious or subconscious channel to the Octarine level. This last point is an important observation, as I do not believe it has been made explicitly clear before in any Chaos Magic text book. The majority of banishing rituals performed by Pagan magickal traditions appear to begin with the opening of a circle, whilst summoning the 'element of ether'. The Pagan understanding of ether is pretty much equivalent to what is called cybermorphic information, or the Octarine level, in this book. They then tend to summon the four elements in such a way that they create a cybermorphic map of the cosmos within their ritual space. In this way, if they are concentrating correctly, they can enter a state of ritual consciousness, creating a group egregor that has a direct channel to the Octarine level. This ritual consciousness is a kind of gnosis. They usually reverse the process at the end of the ritual to end the state of gnosis. When it works, this kind of magic can be

---

[15] Peter J Carroll, *'Liber Kaos'*, (York Beach, ME, 1992), p. 181

very powerful, and I have witnessed some very real magickal effects from working in a group that uses this method.

In Chaos Magic, many different banishing rituals are used, but perhaps the most popular is Carroll's Gnostic Pentagram Ritual, and variations on the theme. This involves vibrating the sounds of the five vowels whilst visualising energy at corresponding points on the body. This is another powerful ritual for entering ritual consciousness, and forming a connection with the Kia.

At the end of a ritual a second banishing ritual is often performed, this time to banish ritual consciousness (as opposed to banishing normal consciousness), but also to act as a release for the spell. Popular among Chaos Magicians is the 'laughter banishing' which involves forced laughter. Since laughter is a magickal emotion and Octarine Gnosis[16], it serves to release any magickal waste, further charging the spell and simultaneously returning the magician(s) to normal consciousness.

It is possible to do magick without a banishing ritual. Such magic will sometimes be auric in nature, which we have already shown may involve a connection directly to the cybermorphic information level, or the ether, or Kia. Sometimes, however magic will fit into neither category. All magic that involves neither, will usually involve some form of gnosis. Gnosis creates a direct link to the cybermorphic level.

All magic, no matter what 'colour', in one way or another involves a direct link to the cybermorphic level. All magic rituals can therefore be said to be at least partially Octarine in nature. This magical information can then be sent directly into the code of the universe to change the programming in such a way that the desired result is obtained.

---

[16] *Carroll, in his Alphabet of Desire, labeled the Solar, Ego gnosis as being 'laughter'. For my sins I have moved this gnosis to the Octarine level, replacing the Solar attribute with Pride (Vanity, Dignity and Arrogance). This is now balanced by the Neptunian attribute of Shame (Embarrassment, Disgrace and Humiliation).*

There is an aspect of banishing rituals which is not Octarine in nature, and this is the aspect that gives these rituals the name 'banishing'. These are most properly associated with the element of Air, Separation Magick and are related to the idea of sacred space. This aspect is discussed in Chapter 4, under Separation Magick.

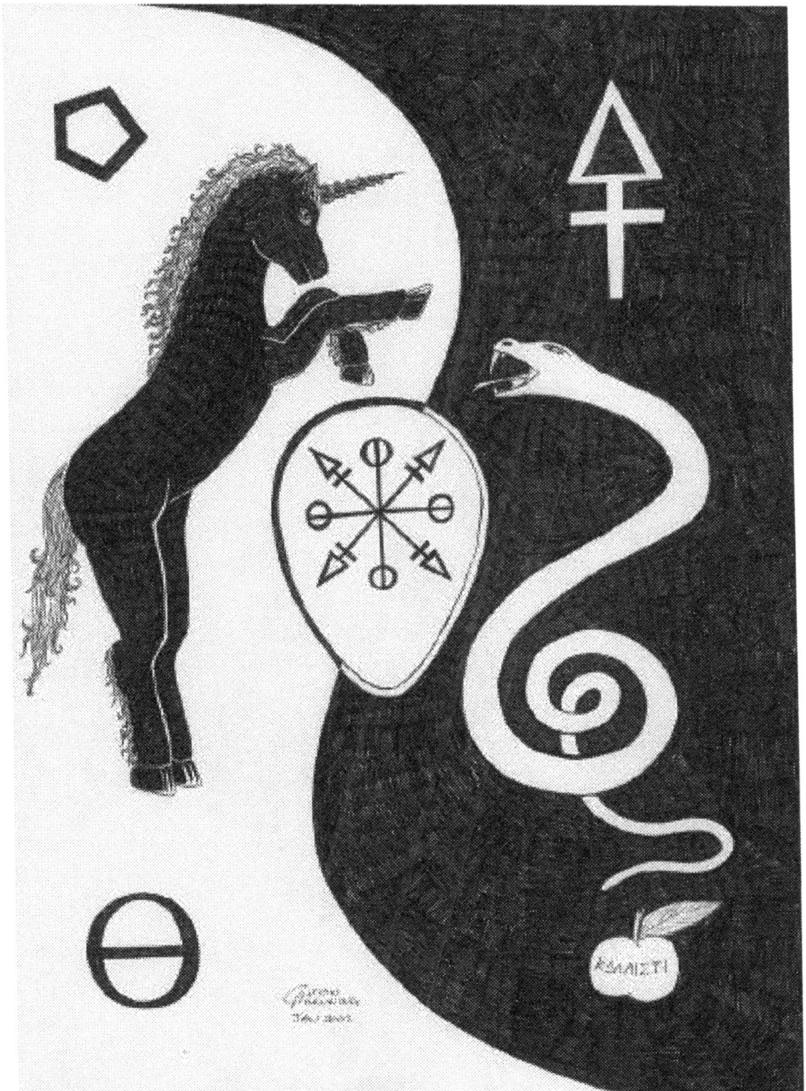
ΚΑΛΛΙΣΤΙ

3. Duality

> 'Some physicists held to the particle theory,
> and insisted that all evidence supporting the wave
> theory would eventually be explained away.
> Others, however, accepted the waves and rejected
> the particles. Still others, somewhat facetiously,
> began talking of 'wavicles.' Bohr suggested that
> the search for one correct model was medieval,
> pre-scientific and obsolete.'
>
> Robert Anton Wilson

Dual Magick is the magick of existence, the magick of balance, the magick of the Yin-Yang, the magick of spirit and soul, doings and beings, waves and particles, processes and objects, instructions and data. It is the magick of defining realities and beliefs. It is also the magic of the sacred chao in Discordianism. Everywhere there is a duality, the interplay of these polarities can be seen to be at work. Forwards and Backwards, Up and Down, Left and Right, Past and Future, our whole world is described in terms of polarities.

It stands to reason therefore, that any magick that we wish to cause visible effects on reality, any results magic, would necessarily concern ourselves with duality. That is not to say that Octarine magic is not used, but more to say that the magic must be directed into an area of duality. Spirit and Soul have been used below to describe the two polarities, but they are in themselves still in a too pure form to have any direct use in results magick. Instead they are described for the purposes of working paradigms for those seeking an alternative to pure magick for a time, and for the purposes of categorising different states of gnosis. Some states of gnosis reach the Kia via the Soul whilst others reach the Kia via the Spirit.

At times a magician may choose to work with a Soul based paradigm, in order to gain knowledge of their being, and of the nature of being. This approach to spirituality has an Eastern bias, and involves stillness and meditation. It is also strongly prevalent in Western transcendental religious belief systems that promote abstinence and an ascetic moral code. Paradoxically it has been the western magickal schools thought generally to be 'left-hand path' that have practised and promoted meditation of this nature. Inhibitory forms of gnosis predominate this paradigm, such as humiliation, terror, release and anger. These forms of gnosis have been used on the masses by religions and states alike in a non-consensual manner for hundreds of years, often to greatly destructive effect. They can be used more positively in a consensual magical environment, and have been by the more 'left-hand path' schools of thought. In recent times most 'right-hand path' schools have tried to deny and anathematise them.

At other times the magician may choose to work with a Spirit based paradigm. This promotes the much more Western idea of doing and activity. Puritanism has adopted a bias towards this paradigm, but because of its strict moral code has chosen to manifest it in a strong 'work ethic'. A more free spirit based paradigm will let it manifest in more hedonistic, pleasure based activities. Meditations of a spirit based nature tend towards pathworkings and other visualisation exercises. Such meditations are favoured by so-called 'right hand path' occult lodges. Excitatory forms of gnosis are favoured in this paradigm, such as orgasm, arrogance, rapture and joy. The establishment has tried to limit and control the extent to which these forms of gnosis are available to the individual, often using extreme forms of punishment on those who disobey. Both right and left hand path magic has made use of these forms of gnosis.

Soul Magick

The Aneristic Principle is that of
APPARENT ORDER...

...Western philosophy is traditionally
concerned with contrasting one grid with another
grid, and amending grids in hopes of finding a
perfect one that will account for all reality and will,
hence, (say unenlightened westerners) be True.
This is illusory; it is what we Erisians call the
ANERISTIC ILLUSION.

Malaclypse the Younger[17]

Soul Magic is concerned with the illusion of being. It is the root of Identity, Resources, Psyche, Ego, Work and Play but is also manifest in the other magics in a more hidden way. Those who follow the path of the Soul, can be said to be following the path of Being. This centres on a belief that there is a perfect unchanging essence to every object, and that the essence is the true nature of the object. Often this essence is referred to as a Soul.

Physics talks about particles. Particles are meant to be solid lumps of mass, often represented as spherical, whizzing about the universe and colliding with other particles. Somehow these miniature marbles, in their whizzing about, were thought by old Newtonian & relativistic scientists to cause the existence of the very universe we experience. These days we can recognise the patent absurdity of this belief, which has an obvious religious undercurrent in the form of a belief in a symmetrical and ordered universe.

That is not to say that particles do not exist, just that they are not what they were thought to be. The observation of particles occurs as a result of examining a particular 'chunk' of the

---

[17] Malaclypse the Younger, *'Principia Discordia; or, How I Found Goddess And What I Did To Her When I Found Her'*, fourth edition (San Francisco, 1970) pp. 49-50

information fabric of existence, and processing it in a particular way. The observation of two or more particles exerting effects upon one another occurs as a result of examining the calculation that occurs when two or more 'chunks' of information are brought together for processing. The fact that they appear as particles is a result of the way the programming works at that level of existence.

So much as things can be said to 'be', they have attributes, or data, 'stored' about them somewhere in the information grid, which is continually accessed and manipulated by functions relating to that data. 'Healing the Soul' is concerned with identifying corrupt data and restoring it to a useful state. The term 'corrupt data' should not be looked upon in a moral sense, but in a computer science sense. When some of your data is meaningless then it is of no use to you, and can even cause some of your functions to crash. Corrupt data may also be inaccurate data, which although valid, are inaccurate and produce resultant actions that are not the most beneficial. A study of 'Soul Magick' is essentially a study of the object information, data, which you currently access concerning yourself and your surroundings, the accuracy and validity of this information and the resultant actions they cause you to make. Fittingly it is a highly reflective and calm type of magick.

The illusion that 'Soul reality' is somehow more real than 'Spirit reality' is the illusion that the universe is ordered. It is what the Discordians have called the Aneristic Illusion. Societies devoted to the Aneristic Illusion have an unhealthy tendency to form a bias for using inhibitory forms of gnosis, including anger, humiliation, release and terror. They tend to view excitatory forms of gnosis, such as orgasm, arrogance, rapture and joy as being 'immoral' to various degrees. We can see this in Christianity, which has a tendency to let its irrational anger get out of control when unchecked, likes to humiliate its victims, terrorise its enemies and 'release' its heretics (through some form of execution, release being the gnosis of death). The Biblical Hebrews and modern day Islamic societies seem little different in this respect. To a fair degree even the Atheist establishment has some of these tendencies, as can be witnessed in the treatment of scientists who propose dissenting views on various subjects. This is not to say that these forms of gnosis should be avoided, just that they should always be kept in balance. Humiliation is especially worth keeping an eye on, as too much of this can lead to an inferiority complex, such as many a megalomaniac dictator has possessed.

Spirit Magick

> The Eristic Principle is that of APPARENT DISORDER...
>
> ...DISORDER is simply unrelated information viewed through a particular grid. But like "relation", no-relation is a concept. Male, like female, is an idea about sex. To say that maleness is "absence of female-ness", or vice versa, is a matter of definition and metaphysically arbitrary. The artificial concept of no-relation is the ERISTIC PRINCIPLE.
>
> The belief that 'order is true' and disorder is false or somehow wrong, is the Aneristic Illusion. To say the same of disorder, is the ERISTIC ILLUSION.
>
> Malaclypse the Younger[18]

Spirit magic is concerned with the illusion of doing. It is the root of Uniting, Dividing, Sex, Death, Love and War, but is also manifest in the other magics in more subtle ways. Those who follow the path of the spirit can be said to be following the path of Doing. Those who follow this path believe that things are only defined by their actions, and that if something is not moving, then it is useless and/or dead. This movement and activity can be called Spirit.

It is noticeable in a religion such as Christianity that cults that

---

[18] Malaclypse the Younger, *'Principia Discordia; or, How I Found Goddess And What I Did To Her When I Found Her'*, fourth edition (San Francisco, 1970) pp. 49-50

emphasise the soul prefer inhibitory forms of gnosis, quiet meditation and reflection, self flagellation and penance, whilst those that emphasise the 'Holy Spirit' are more prone to ecstatic states of excitatory gnosis. This is because Spirit is something that can be contacted only through a total state of action and complete denial of being, whilst the soul is something that can only be reached by stilling the self into a state where one is totally focused on ones being, with little or no doing taking place.

A true Spirit based cult would over-emphasise the importance of Orgasm, Arrogance, Rapture and Joy, whilst trying to suppress all forms of Terror, Anger, Humiliation and Release to various degrees. This can be seen to be the case in the New Age movement in general, where 'Politically Correct' views are arrogantly asserted and practised, regardless of whether these views actually make sense, orgasm and free-love were generously supported up until the AIDS scare, and where even now tantra and other forms of sexual yoga are very much practised. Everyone is meant to go around Joyful all the time and many are 'enraptured' by their favourite gurus and/or deities. A New-Ager is likely to see Terror, Anger, Humiliation and Release as undesirable and to be avoided. The term 'bad vibes' used to be used to describe these emotions, but the more modern 'negative energies' differs little in meaning. 'Bad karma' is also spoken of in this context. It is amusing to observe that one cult's 'dark side' is almost exactly the other cults 'light side' and vice versa.

Modern physics has begun to detect and observe the phenomena of Spirit, which it calls wave functions. Some physicists are beginning to think that these 'waves' are the 'real' reality and what we know as particles are actually only manifest as a result of the waves. The magic of Carroll is based on the manipulation of these 'probability' waves, which probably accounts for the Doing bias found in his work. Despite Carroll's dislike of the New Age, his roots seem to be in the same type of paradigm, a spirit based paradigm. It has manifested in a different way in Carroll as a result of his different philosophical and psychological make-up. Despite his doing bias, there are many characteristics in his books that are more typical of a being type system. In fact the chaos magic system presented by Carroll is surprisingly well balanced, despite his obvious prejudices. I hope that my work in this book has further helped to establish/develop the balanced holistic system that Chaos Magick and other contemporary systems of sorcery have brought to us.

All through history there have been those who have reached a balanced understanding of things, and have been well balanced in themselves, healthy in spirit and soul. Some such have tried to explain it and formed cults, others have tried to hide it in occult writings, fearing that the knowledge would be dangerous to those who didn't understand, and those that weren't even aware of their own understanding and who just got on with their lives. Magicians have begun to realise that the strange occult writings, the misleading cults and unawareness can all be just as dangerous in the hands of the ignorant as if the teachings were freely available in an easy to understand form. Of course, years of conditioning in the occult world is hard to break, and many books, even this one, will contain much technical jargon that will not be understood by all. Many modern books that seem easy to understand have been over simplified, are essentially vague and are actually more misleading than useful, although it is possible to extract useful information from them if you know what you are looking for.

The Eristic Illusion has been based on the theory of wave functions, or its contemporary counterpart, throughout human history. Today the theory that the universe is built up out of insubstantial but powerful wave formations that combine to produce the illusion of the solid world we witness is both exciting and terrifying. It is the first hint that the world we live in is not as ordered as it was once thought. However, to focus entirely on this aspect of reality and to insist that it is somehow 'more true' than the ordered illusion previously dominant is just as much of an error. The error is caused by selectively only observing the processes that occur and defining even objects as being 'made up of processes'. But if objects are actually made of processes then the processes themselves become meaningless. If a process is something that manipulates, or changes the data of an object, but there aren't actually any objects or data except those defined by yet more processes, then eventually at the bottom level you find pure unadulterated information, information that describes both the data and the processes, but in its most pure form the two are indistinguishable.

The Alchemical Trinity

What is the fundamental reality of this Universe? Is it matter - solid 'mater', the Great Mother, the feminine 'yin' principle? Is it energy - the dynamic, masculine 'yang' principle, or 'God'? Or is it information - the hermaphroditic Mercurius, or Tao, as one-dimensional 'strings' of data?

Ramsey Dukes[19]

If one were to combine the magics of Duality discussed in this chapter with the Pure Magic described in the previous chapter then one may well arrive at a system that has much in common with the alchemical system of threes. This system was made up of Mercury, Sulphur and Salt. The Mercury in this system was different from the planetary Mercury of astrology. The planets represented aspects of both the macrocosm and microcosm and the alchemist saw them as energies out of balance. The alchemists did not reject astrology out of hand as has Pete Carroll, but then neither did they blindly accept it. The whole purpose of the alchemical process was to combine the energies of the seven classical planets within the microcosm, (Uranus, Neptune and Pluto having been discovered more recently) in order to gain rulership over all twelve signs of the zodiac. Each of the seven planets ruled two of the twelve signs, except the Sun and Moon which both only ruled one. The seven planets were special alchemical symbols made from a mixture of four symbols, which represented the four elements. These four symbols were the cross, arrow, crescent and circle, which represented the sword (air), the wand (fire), the cup (water) and the pentacle (earth) respectively. If we examine the symbols of the seven planets we can confirm that they do indeed appear to be made exclusively from combinations of these four symbols.

---

[19] Ramsey Dukes, *'Words Made Flesh'*, (Wharf Mill, 1988), back cover

62

The alchemists chose to represent 'their Mercury' or 'higher Mercury' as containing all four of these symbols, something none of the planetary symbols can claim. The Monas Hieroglyph of Dr John Dee, taken from his work Monas Hieroglyphica[20] is a more stylised form of this symbol for Mercury, surrounded by an egg. Eggs are another alchemical symbol of Mercury. The diagram below shows how Alchemical Mercury contains a balance of all elements and therefore a transcendence of the planetary energies, which are made from partial combinations of the elements. Salt and Sulphur both only combine two elements, and contain none in common.

---

[20] *English title:- "The Hieroglyphic Monad"*

Salt
Circle +
Crescent[21]

Mercury
Crescent +
Circle +
Cross +
Arrow

Sulphur
Arrow +
Cross

Sun	Moon	Mars	Mercury	Jupiter	Venus	Saturn
Circle + Circle	Crescent	Circle + Arrow	Crescent + Circle + Cross	Crescent + Cross	Circle + Cross	Cross + Crescent

Mercury corresponds with the Ether, or Pure Magick in the Kaosphere system, the point where all duality has been transcended, 'truth' and 'falsehood' included, and anything is possible. Salt and Sulphur relate to the magics of duality described in this chapter, Salt representing 'Being' and Sulphur representing 'Doing'. Salt represents Earth and Water, Mass and Time. This is akin to the view of 'objects' moving in 'time', the ordered Aneristic Illusion. Sulphur represents Fire and Air, Energy and Space, the Eristic Illusion of 'waves' moving through emptiness. Mercury is the mass of information that describes

---

[21] *The Crescent is less visible in Salt than any of the four symbols appear in the alchemical glyphs. The central line is in fact a crescent, and should be visualised in three dimensions, the 'line' arcing out of the page like a crescent on its side.*

both simultaneously, where concepts such as space, time, mass and energy don't exist except in description. If binary were the language you would only see a stream of 0s and 1s, nothing would tell you what was 'space' and what was 'time'. For this reason it is here that the universe fractal may be changed in subtle ways using magickal manipulation and it has always been the goal of the magician to attain a balance at this spot. Not that the balance sought by a magician is static like that of a mystic. From such a position of equilibrium the magician seeks to re-immerse into duality to experience the richness the world offers, as opposed to the mystic who retreats to a position of equilibrium in order to escape from reality.

The realms of the planetary energies have much pleasure to offer those willing to taste of their fruits, and the illuminated magician will waste no time in using their advantage to taste of them fully. The only real purpose of the high 'spiritual' magick of self-transformation is to give one a better vantage point from which to use results magic to make the most of 'the Chaos of the Normal', to borrow Spare's phrase.

The Formula of Three

It is possible to make a neat little magickal formula from these three alchemical concepts. You begin with the Salt, which symbolises the Earth as it is in its current state. Before performing any kind of magic, a wise magician will work out precisely what it is that they want changed.

Once the magician has worked out what they want, they formulate this into a 'statement of intent'. This is the magicians 'Will' and corresponds to Sulphur. Merely projecting your Will at the world is unlikely to have much effect however, as anyone who has ever tried to bend a spoon with will-power will have discovered.

The third stage is the stage of gnosis. The magician attempts to enter the realm where their 'Will' and the 'World' are indistinguishable, and thus implant their 'Will' into the 'World' in the way a computer hacker may insert a virus or alteration into a computer program. This is the realm of Mercury.

What precipitates is the result. This is a 'new' Salt, the resulting World. If the magician was successful then this new world will now contain the desired improvement. If the magician failed then it may have been changed in an unexpected way, an

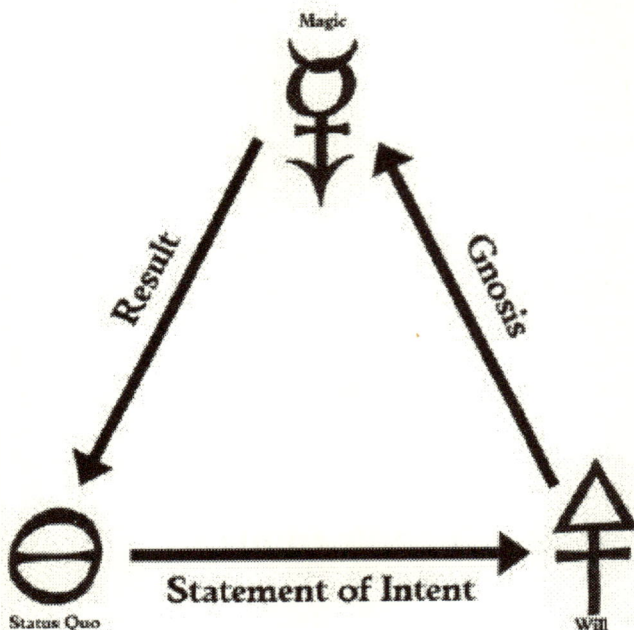

unnoticed way or may simply be unchanged. Whatever the case, the magician will notice some other change they wish to make and the process can start over again.

The wise magician will not get to obsessed with this control, for your own pleasure and well being there need to be times when you sit back and simply go with the flow, in order to enjoy what you have achieved so far, as Dave Lee points out in Chaotopia[22]...

> Magick is defined as : causing change to occur in conformity with will, expanding your achievable reality, the pursuit of power, and so on.
> All these definitions presuppose control as the central theme in magick. This is all fine and good, but it illustrates that magick cannot address issues outside of the sphere of control. These are issues that are usually chunked up into mysticism, and neglected or anathematised by Chaos magicians. This is a mistake, because the half of our quality of experience is dependent upon our ability to let go, stop worrying, stop controlling and enjoy.

---

[22] Dave Lee, *'Chaotopia'* (Leeds, 1997), p. 13

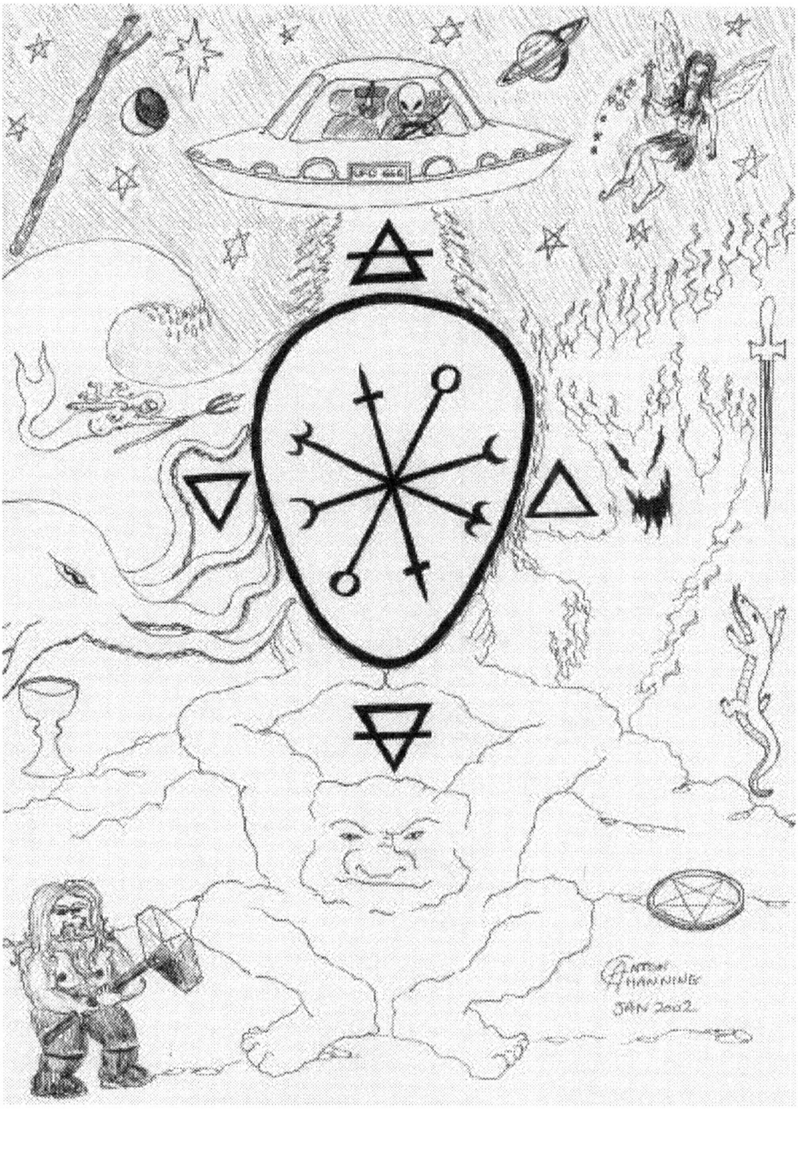
ANTON CHANNING
JAN 2002

4. Elemental Magick

Call them what you will, I believe that the
spirits of natural, and some things which would
seem at first as not natural, exist whether or not
we choose to believe in them. These elemental
spirits are very much a part of our world, which
we cannot afford to ignore or dismiss if we are to
understand our own magical nature, or that which
draws us into the world of magic.

Jaq D. Hawkins[23]

The four elements of Earth, Water, Fire and Air are
probably the best known aspects of Western magic. I was first
taught about them in a Roman Catholic school, in a GCSE
History class, studying the history of medicine, which covered the
topic of the 'four humours'. I had also encountered them many
times in fiction, including Advanced Dungeons and Dragons role-
playing games. Since studying magick, I have been struck by the
way many authors disagree over the correspondences of Fire and
Air. Most authors largely agree concerning the attribution of the
Sensual, Practical and Common Sense Physical world of Earth
and the Emotional, Caring, but sometimes Moody and Brooding
world of Water. But there seems to be a large divide concerning
the correspondences of Air and Fire. This divide is not an issue I
wish to involve myself in, but inevitably in a chapter devoted to a
cursory discussion of the four elements, my own prejudices will
show through.

I request that if the reader finds my elemental attributions
'incorrect', that they ignore the words 'Fire' and 'Air' and instead
concentrate on the concepts of 'Identity' and 'Separation', which
are far more important to my discussion than some ancient
medieval symbols in any case. If you find these chapters make
more sense to you if you associate 'Fire' with separation and 'Air'
with identity, then by all means do so.

---

[23] Jaq D Hawkins *'Spirits of the Earth'* (Chieveley, 1998), p. 7

I have included some brief discussion concerning the idea of elemental spirits, a common theme in many magical traditions, but my comments on these spirits are by no means meant to be definitive. I have included the descriptions I have should they prove useful and/or challenging to the way the reader thinks about or approaches such spirits. For an in depth study of elemental spirits from the perspective of a magician, the reader is directed to read the 'Spirits of the Elements' series by Jaq D Hawkins. This series devotes a whole book to each element and covers ground inspirational for any serious magician wishing to work with the elemental spirits of the classical elements.

In terms of the kaosphere cybermorph, the level of the four elements can be a useful area of magic in which to work. It seems to categorise objects and operations in a neat and tidy way, if that is what is required. It would appear that it is the level of reality that ordinary, non-magicians operate on, in terms of individual consciousness. It is neither the hyper-real ecstatic states of consciousness found in the eight colours, normal to the enlightened magician, nor is it the 'super-natural' or 'spiritual' bliss found at the levels of Soul, Spirit and Kia, a familiar feeling for magicians and mystics, experienced in intense meditation and states of gnosis. The direct experience of the Kaos Unmanifest is something so far removed from ordinary consciousness that I would not be surprised to learn that it has driven many insane when they have accidentally tapped this awesome and powerful state of consciousness. It would appear that the four elements are the divisions of ordinary day-to-day consciousness for the vast majority of people living in the industrial aeon. Since the Western world in which we live is currently moving beyond industry and into the new aeon of information, I would expect that more and more ordinary people will begin shifting their consciousness into a system of eight. These will include the eight colours, the pagan wheel of the year, Dr Timothy Leary's eight circuits and the eight Chinese trigrams among other systems. Before the industrial age, many people lived their ordinary lives in the dualistic realms of Salt and Sulphur. It would seem that consciousness is becoming more and more fragmented, or at least that it is becoming self-aware of an already existing fragmentation, and as it does so more and more freedom is gained, both collectively and individually. Already the four elements are coming to be seen as mystical and spiritual, instead of the hyper-real materialism they must have appeared to the average monotheist alchemist.

It is possible that the four elements need a make-over, new names, new correspondences. After all there are many ideas and concepts used to describe the Aether, Spirit and Soul. There are few, if any ideas that replace the four elements, although it could be possible to dig up the four humours, or make more of Carroll's Mass, Energy, Time and Space analogy. As a result the ideas the four elements are trying to map have become obscured by the map itself, so that many magicians have come to see Earth, Air, Fire and Water as magical fact, rather than as a fairly good magical map. This is a more deeply ingrained and deep-rooted problem than even the confusion of qabala with 'magical truth', although the problem is more common in the wider magickal community than in Chaos Magic, where the eight colours have become the normal mode of perception and classification. It is also a problem that is less often questioned. For this reason, I have also decided to include Carroll's 'new' four elements in the correspondences of this chapter, to provide an alternative to the over-used classical map of the four-fold division.

Also briefly discussed under each element are the four magickal operations associated with the elements. The fifth magickal operation, Illumination, is an operation of Octarine, Aetheric magick. These are included in the chapter for purposes of completion, and the serious reader should also refer to the excellent 'Sleight of Mind' chapters in Carroll's Liber Kaos.

Fire *(Energy)* - Identity Magick

Your hearts know in silence
the secrets of the days and nights.
But your ears thirst
for the sound of your heart's knowledge.
You would know in words
that which you have always known in thought.
You would touch with your fingers
the naked body of your dreams.
And it is well you should.
Kahlil Gibran

Identity Magick is magic concerned with beings, in particular it is concerned with the self being as opposed to other beings. By examining what it is that constitutes the 'self' it is possible to get a clearer understanding of the nature of being. What is your being? What is your identity? Is it your body? Surely your body is a part of your identity in some senses, but if you lost part of it in an accident, would you lose your identity? The identity of all beings is just as mutable as the identity of the self.

Identity Magic is essentially that magic which is concerned with those aspects the self that can be considered neither a part of our ego, nor a part of our psyche. In another sense it can be understood to be related to those parts of the self which manifest in both the ego and the psyche. It is the magic of your personal Soul (or Souls), alienated from the Souls of things around you. Your body may be considered to be a part of your identity, depending on how you are choosing to look at it at any one time, it may also be viewed as separate from you, part of the resources at your disposal. If your body worries you in any way then it may even relate to the psyche, or if you use it to create an impression then it is part of your ego.

Normally the body can be seen as an important part of your identity, but it is by no means all of it. There will be certain things that you enjoy doing, or that you and others identify with yourself, that are neither a part of your psyche nor reflected directly in your ego. Identities that are adopted are essentially those parts of the self that can occupy both the psyche and the ego. When an identity is called to outward expression it becomes part of the ego, otherwise it goes to rest in the psyche. As such it can neither be considered a permanent part of the ego or of the psyche, it is something which dances between the two.

A man who wears leathers and hangs out in rock bars, his long hair draping over his shoulders most nights, but during the working week wears a suit and tie, has his hair in a pony tail and is a respected professional, is an example of someone using identities. When not at work his 'rocker' image becomes part of the ego, and his 'work persona' retreats back into the psyche. When at work the reverse is true. Some of his acquaintances might be fully aware of both identities, and will often respect him all the more for it.

Identity magic is partly concerned with the pursuit of self-knowledge, partly concerned with the development of new identities, but is also concerned with the identities of others. If you move the perspective of self to someone else, see yourself as one of their 'others', you can begin to understand how that individual identifies themselves, beyond what is normally apparent from their outward persona. The outward persona, or ego, is that part of the self which pretends to be other beings' 'others'. When you see someone's ego you see them how they want the outside world to see them. If you can see through this and identify the identities behind the masks, you can see how they want to see themselves. This is arguably not as useful as being able to see how you want to see yourself. If you don't properly understand your own identities then it is unlikely you will have anything more than a very distorted image of anyone else's.

Invocation
The magickal operation known as invocation is concerned with the development of new identities. This is most commonly performed by 'summoning' a deity from a preferred pantheon 'into' the recipient. During the ritual the magician in possession will have taken on the identity of the chosen deity. Although the deity is usually banished, it is likely that something will remain inside the magician, that they will be transformed by the experience in some way. A more permanent identity change can

be achieved with a different kind of invocation. In this case the magician does a series of rituals to draw the identity of the chosen deity into themselves over a long period of time, until they can eventually feel like they have 'become' that deity. This can also be performed using characters from various stories, films, and/or TV series. A pop idol, alive or dead, or famous film star, can also be used. The principle is the same in each case. It is important to have a clear idea which attributes of the character you are trying to acquire, otherwise you might end up with something quite other than what you bargained for.

Fire Elementals

Elementals of the element of Fire have been known in traditional magic as 'salamanders', mythical lizards thought to be capable of living only in the flames of a blazing fire. The elementals of this element do not all appear to be salamanders however. Some take on the appearance of a phoenix, others look like the devils that stoke the fires of Hell. Some, known as devlins, take on the appearance of manlike things made entirely of fire. It is generally thought that a flame needs to be burning for one to be present, although in practise fire is only symbolic of what they represent and no flame is actually necessary.

Different fire elementals would appear to have different specialities and characteristics. The phoenix is a specialist at total transformation of identity. Salamanders are more general purpose. The devils have a mischievous character, whilst the devlins tend towards a very aggressive nature. Fire elementals are by no means limited to those mentioned above, and if you can't find reference to one in some mythology or fantasy story that suits your needs, then it should be a simple task to custom build an elemental to your own requirements. Children's stories and games often contain useful characters for these purposes. Charmander, Growlithe, Vulpix and Ponyta are useful fire-spirits from the popular children's card game known as Pokemon[24].

---

[24] Since writing that sentence, a Pokemon craze has come and gone, leaving cartoons, films, computer games, toys and an unending list of merchandise in its wake.

It might be useful to obtain a general purpose fire elemental in the form of a lantern, one that uses night-light style candles. There are many magickal paradigms where 'calling the quarters' is performed as part of the opening banishing ritual. In 'calling the quarters' an elemental of each of the four types is summoned, each element usually represented by some physical object, such as a lantern for Fire, a rock for Earth, a lit incense burner for air and a bowl of water for Water. The advantage of such a lantern is that it can be used in out of doors rituals without the wind blowing it out.

In Tarot the element of fire is represented by the suit of wands or rods. However the magickal operation of invocation is more usually associated with the magickal weapon of the sword. This discrepancy has occurred as a result of two separate magickal traditions evolving conflicting correspondences. Modern magicians have to choose whether to work with one or both of these variants. As such a wand, staff or sword can be considered a special type of fire elemental, or anything else that you have chosen to represent the operations of these weapons, such as a ring or knife. As a result there is also an ambiguity concerning the correspondence of fire to identity magic. You may prefer to correspond fire to separation magic, and to the magical operation of enchantment. The case for fire symbolising enchantment links fire to our imagination, a word whose root is significantly linked to the words magic and making. Enchantment is the magic of making what we have visualised in our imagination come to be, in other words willing what is perceived. Such is the ambiguity exhibited by the elements of fire and air. I have chosen to correspond identity magic with fire, and separation magic with air. Each magician to their own.

76

Earth *(Mass)* - Resources Magick

To you the earth yields fruit,
and you shall not want
if you but know how to fill your hands.
It is in exchanging the gifts of the earth
that you shall find abundance and be satisfied.
Yet unless the exchange be in love
and kindly justice
it will but lead some to greed
and others to hunger.
Kahlil Gibran

Because the new cybermorphic system has revealed significant inconsistencies in the old system of 'Wealth Magic', it is necessary for us undertake an exploration of the newly revealed significance of Resources Magic, how it differs from the old Wealth Magick, what it tells us about what we were doing right, what it tells us about what we were doing wrong and what it suggests we should be aiming for in future when we are trying to be successful in this area of magick.

Resources Magic concerns beings, as opposed to doings. Specifically it concerns other beings, as opposed to the self being. Other beings includes, but is not limited to, other humans, animals, inanimate objects, your own body, tools, toys, the environment in which we live, money and time. It concerns all aspects of how we relate to the other beings, including how we accumulate them, organise them and use them as tools (Work), how we store them, preserve them and use them for storage (Rest) and how we spend, consume or use them as toys and/or for pleasure (Play). Thus it encompasses, but is not limited to, the two extremes of Work Magic and Play Magic. In short, Resources Magic helps you Work, Rest and Play! Work and Play magick can be considered separate magicks in their own right, and are explored in detail in the eight colours of magick chapter. Resources Magick is about how well you have attained a balance between Working, Resting and Playing, and about how well this balance achieves the manipulation of resources that you want it to.

The aim of Resources Magick is to become resourceful. To

be resourceful one needs to be able to organise, manipulate, gather and use the resources at your disposal in a way which makes best use of them. Old style Wealth Magic concentrates almost exclusively on how one used resources for pleasure, play. It briefly mentions the importance of the process of gathering/accumulating wealth and ignores completely what you should do with resources that are not immediately of use. In short, what old Wealth Magic actually does is arrange, organise and manipulate your existing resources so that you get maximum pleasure potential out of them. This is a way of organising your life for nothing but play. What is more, for most of us this process on its own becomes a stumbling block, a real obstacle to gaining real wealth. It makes us feel like we are pleased and content, but really it makes us easily pleased and content to be poor. This is of course a useful ability, but it is only one third of the picture.

What you do with your resources when you don't yet need them is an important part of resourcefulness. Unfortunately it is one much overlooked by most texts concerning wealth magic, which often explain in great detail how money is dead unless it is in circulation. Resources which are kept in storage are not dead, they're just resting. Any squirrel will tell you how useful it is to keep a store of things you won't need until later.

What then are the essential elements of successfully storing things? I would suggest three things, security, preservation and ease of retrieval. Things may well be preserved and secure in an air tight box kept buried in a fifty foot hole on the planet Pluto, but you're not going to be able to access it yourself very easily either. It could take you more work to store and later retrieve the resources than it took you to collect the resources in the first place. Unless the resources have changed in respect of how easy they are to replace, you shouldn't use any storage system that requires more work to store and later retrieve the resources than it took to get the resources in the first place. In practice it will be preferable if the amount of effort required to store and retrieve resources kept in storage is next to zero, unnoticeable when compared to the effort required to gain them.

Sometimes it is possible to store things in such a way that

your resources multiply whilst in storage, depending on the nature of the resources themselves. Organic life, such as plants, fungi, seeds, animals and money, can all reproduce in the correct environment. You will need to research the environment best suited to your resource and your needs. In such a case it may be worth considering a storage system which requires a little more effort in storage and retrieval. You will need to weigh up the extra effort against the expected benefits before deciding. There may also be other advantages. In the case of vegetables, if you store them in a vegetable garden or allotment, in order to grow them and have them reproduce, then you can avoid using poisons and inorganic fertilisers, without having to pay the hefty prices normally paid for organic produce. Such advantages will again have to be weighed up against any extra work. If such an option has all the advantages, yet requires less work, then you are laughing!

Rest magic is any magic dedicated to improving the security of stored resources, improving the size and/or quality of a storage space and/or improving the preservation of stored resources. In other words magic concerned with the protection of resources from theft and/or decay and making sure there is enough room for them. In the case of human/animal resources it can also be concerned with making sure they don't escape. Children, for example, need to be carefully prevented from wandering off and getting lost and/or damaged when you aren't watching them, especially when they are being stored outside. Cats are quite independent but have an unfortunate tendency to wander off into busy roads where they can be killed. If you have a cat, and are a magician, it is likely that it is also your familiar and therefore a very important magickal resource, in addition to the usual pleasure resource one would normally attribute to pets. Some animals are also working animals, which makes them tool resources. Slavery has been abolished, but if it hadn't been then making sure your slaves didn't escape was an important part of owning them, similarly with serfs.

This day and age has more subtle forms of slavery, such as debt, employment and nationality. Banks and mortgage lenders try to ensure that no-one escapes making the payments that give them profits. All creditors consider their debtors to be important resources. The debtors are trapped into a system where they have to work to pay off their debts. Employers need to make sure they don't lose their important human resources, otherwise the running of the business will suffer. Employees entirely dependant on financial reward are easy to keep, unless another employer can offer them more. Nations like to keep a hold of their populations and make sure they stay put and don't move around. In this way it is easier for taxes to be collected. The artificial concepts of 'nationality' and 'immigration' are the governments' ways of enslaving people to particular areas.

Slaves and serfs are not the only type of human resources, nor are they the most useful. Your friends are actually an important human resource, probably amongst the most important. After all, how resourceful are you if you can't even keep your friends. Friendship is hard work, but is also very rewarding in terms of the fun and pleasure you can experience with them. A real friend is someone you can work, rest and play with, although in practise you may find you have different friends for all three. How to win and keep friends is more a part of ego magic, specifically charisma and leadership and will be discussed under that chapter, but it is important to note at this stage that the reason it is important to be able to do so is because having friends is an important and powerful resource in life.

If you do lose an important resource, even a special friend or human resource, then it is important to grieve this loss but not to dwell too long on it. Having made such a drastic loss it is important to get on and see what you can do to replace that loss. Far from being disrespectful to the thing lost, replacing it will show how much it was valued, to the extent that another resource was needed in its place. Replacing it with nothing could actually be saying that it wasn't actually worth anything to you, and that your tears are more from guilt. Although in a lot of cases nothing will be able to replace an important human or animal resource perfectly, due to each human and animals unique nature, the fact that they meant something to you, means that you were getting something from them that was of benefit to you, such as some emotional need that they helped satisfy. That emotional need will still need satisfaction, and it is important for your own health and wellbeing that you find some way of reconciling this. This can be done by either freeing yourself of the need, by replacing it with a different need, or by finding something else that satisfies the existing need.

The environment is another important resource, and one we share not just with other humans, but with all the plant and animal life of the planet. There are many ways of ensuring this resource is not diminished, polluted and destroyed but they are beyond the scope of this chapter, and indeed this book. Needless to say that buying organic food from a supermarket is scratching at the surface and doesn't really address he issues. Organic box schemes, growing your own produce in a garden/allotment, recycling everything you can, buying locally grown produce, cycling, walking and using public transport in order to avoid using cars, not supporting businesses known to exploit the environment can all add up to not only a much more fulfilling and healthy life-style, but can also help preserve the environment in which you live. Personally I am an optimist concerning humankind's probable future, and believe that we will eventually build a world that runs on sustainable principles, individual freedom, respect for the natural chaos of the Earth and an end to militaristic nationalism. This is not some kind of Utopia and it will not be a paradise free of all problems, but the people of that time will look back to the year 2000[25] with the same mixture of romance and disgust that we have when looking back at Victorian society. We are generally disgusted at the social conditions of the poor in our own country at that time. The future world will be amazed and disgusted at the social conditions of the poor in our own world at this time, since they will take for granted whatever solutions they have found to that particular problem.

Evocation

The magickal operation associated with the element of Earth is that of evocation. The magickal weapon is the pentacle, so named because its most common appearance has a pentagram engraved upon it. In fact a pentacle can have any symbol that symbolises the cosmos, macrocosm and microcosm, on it. It can be as simple or as complex as you feel comfortable with. Those particularly interested in Chaos Magic, for example, will probably like to use a pentacle that has a chaosphere image upon it.

Pentacles are usually disks, but they don't have to be. The puzzle cube from the Hellraiser films is a good example of a variant on an evocation tool. Although the cube in the films seems a bit limited, in terms of the spirits that can be summoned, and the ability of the magician to control what happens, it should be possible to make a more useful variant of this device[26].

A good magician does not actually need to have a pentacle,

---

[25] *The year in which I am writing this chapter.*

[26] *Warning! This suggestion has not been tested. The author will not be held responsible for an accidental summoning of Pinhead.*

they contain the map inside their head, but it is useful in more ceremonial rituals, and it is aesthetically pleasing to have one. A tarot deck is often considered to be a divination tool, and hence a magical weapon correspondent with the cup and water. However, tarot cards do not have to be used as a divination device. A complete tarot deck can be considered to be a very comprehensive cosmological map, and each card is symbolic of a different spirit that may be evoked. Used in this way a tarot deck can make a very powerful pentacle. The fact that they can also be used in enchantment and invocation, as well as visualisation exercises and pathworkings, makes them one of the best portable magickal tools available to the magician. The magickal equivalent of a 'Swiss army knife'.

Earth Elementals

Elementals of Earth can be of particular use in resource magic. They can be seen as a special type of spirit or servitor concerned with helping in matters of resources. Freed from the out-dated paradigm that concerns the element of earth with only material resources, we can give them the power to help us with all our resource needs, such as the accumulation of a needed practical skill, or the acquisition of a favour owed. Or even the development of a more powerful and/or healthy body resource.

Traditionally these elementals are called 'gnomes', although it can safely be assumed that there are many other types. Dwarves are a similar kind to gnomes. Trolls are quite different. Golems and gargoyles are also very much connected with stone materials and can thus be considered earth elementals, unless they have been specifically created for some other purpose. All of these things have special individual properties, and you should select one best suited to your particular needs. If you want gold (money), then a gnome would be a useful servitor. Physical strength and bodily health might be better served with a troll. A dwarf is considered both a lover of gold, a good miner, and renowned for their physical strength and constitution. As great smiths they can be of great use in the construction of magical weapons, artefacts and talismans. Like fire elementals, if you can't find a suitable variant within myth or fantasy, feel free to create your own special earth elemental. It is bound to exist on some plane of existence, or can be pulled out of the non-existence.

Air *(Space)* - Separation Magick

Invisibility is an art of moving through time and space. One has to remember that visibility requires an observer. Some people become invisible by blending into a crowd or by making themselves so outrageous by look or behaviour that nobody takes any notice. My own favourite method of invisibility is to sense the exact moment when I can walk through a place, especially a busy public place, when nobody will be looking. Their attention is distracted for just a few seconds simultaneously by various causes and like Obiwan Kenobi traversing the Death Star right under the noses of many storm troopers who happen to be looking the other way, I pass through, for all intents and purposes, invisibly.

Jaq D Hawkins[27]

Separation Magic is magic that is concerned with doings, or processes. Specifically it is concerned with dividing processes. This kind of magic can have a multitude of diverse uses, ranging from invisibility, banishing, protection spells, and spells to ward off particular influences. The two extremes of separation, sex and death, are dealt with separately[28] in their respective parts of the chapter on the eight colours of magic.

An invisibility spell is concerned with removing oneself, or a particular object, from other peoples attention, often whilst the subject is in plain view. This is most useful in the protection of objects from theft, and in the diverting of attention from objects lying about your home you may not wish all visitors to see. Most magicians will have whole collections of books, artefacts and pictures decorating their home, which may come under this description. The avoidance of inviting persons into your home

---

[27] Jaq D Hawkins, *'Chaos Monkey'*, (Milverton, 2002) pp. 163-4

[28] *Appropriately enough.*

85

you do not wish to show such matters is an easy way to avoid this situation, as is being totally out of the closet and building a reputation as such an outrageous magician that people would be disappointed not to see such things in your home. Such extremes are not always practical. Some magicians in the profession of private part-time teaching have students attend their home for lessons. Since the magicians earnings are dependant upon retaining students, the last thing the magician needs is to have to explain their beliefs to their clientele. A lot of good business can be lost that way. Spells concerned with the separation of these objects from people's selective attention are more effective than one might realise. People are usually more than willing to only notice things they expect to see.

Personal invisibility is a different matter, and is usually very effective if performed using mundane and psychological means alone. The first approach is to dress in a manner entirely ordinary in every sense of the word, although this may still leave you entirely visible to those who know you. The other extreme is to dress in outrageous costume, to the extent that although people will notice you, they will be too afraid to acknowledge you for fear that you may be mad. This is illustrated by the famous tale of Crowley performing 'invisibility' whilst wearing bright saffron robes and walking around London. As the story goes he used to enter a gentleman's coffee house and perform Egyptian chants. The polite gentlemen that frequented the venue said nothing and gave Crowley not so much as a glance, although they were no doubt physically able to 'see' and 'hear' Crowley, they prevented themselves from actually taking any notice of their senses. There is a story that says a young man had just started work at this particular venue, and on seeing Crowley perform asked his boss what was going on. His boss simply replied 'Oh don't worry about that, it's just Mr Crowley being invisible again.' in a calm matter-of-fact voice. Whether this was success or failure for Crowley, I leave up to the reader to determine.

Banishing is a very common theme in magic, and one associated with the weapon of the sword. It is in this sense that the sword is associated with the element of Air, and this sword of reason and banishing should not be confused with the sword of fire and invocation. Similarly the wand has two aspects, one of fire and identity, the other of air and inspiration. Psychic manifestation has a way of disappearing in front of a rational mind, or at least becoming temporarily invisible. It is fitting therefore that a magician should use the tool of reason, a sword of air, to banish unwanted phenomena and to clear unwanted psychic energy before and after a ritual. This is usually performed whilst simultaneously raising consciousness to the Octarine level, or the personal Kia, as described in chapter 2, under the section on Banishing Rituals.

Protection spells and spells to ward off particular influences are similar in many ways to invisibility and banishing rituals, although protection may well involve the threat of retribution. If the object in need of protection is a possession, then we can see some overlap with resource magic where part of that magic is concerned with ensuring resources are secure. The combination of resource magic security and separation magic protection can be viewed as being akin to the combination of a safe for security and a guard for protection. For most purposes a purpose built servitor serves as excellent protection. For several years of my life I lived in insecure housing, with no lock on my bedroom door and sharing a house with strangers, many of whom were not averse to thieving. For much of my stay a protection servitor prevented anything from going missing, and it was only when I was moving out that suddenly some items were stolen. I had a good idea who was responsible although I did not pursue the matter at the time. It was only later that I discovered that the thief had become an unwitting victim of my protection servitor, smashing up windows of the house claiming he could see demonic faces staring back at him. At that moment I decided to weigh up what I had lost and how much I had made him pay for it, and decided his debt was paid. I called the demon off. Although he now no longer sees this entity, he is still very much effected by his experience and is far from what anyone could call mentally balanced, but how he chooses to interpret his experiences are his own responsibility and I have no regrets in using such a servitor.

At times a magician will need to specifically ward off an unwanted influence that has entered their life, or someone else's life, or some object/place. To do this is very similar to a general banishing ritual, although more emphasis is put on banishing the specific unwanted influence. The raising of energy through various states of gnosis will assist this, and although the 'rage' gnosis of War Magic can be effective, one needs to be aware that the objective in this case is not the confrontation of War Magick, but separation, the warding off of the unwanted influence. It will not always be a person one may wish to ward off. It may be the warding off of birds from a field of crops, or warding off junk mail from your post. Sometimes an invoked deity will stay persistently in possession of a magician in a ritual, and in such a case another magician will usually act quickly to banish the deity which has become an 'unwanted influence'. In all cases the object is to remove, or separate from the subject the unwanted influence.

The other aspect of the element of Air or Space, is that of rationalism, or the classification and categorisation of facts. This is often known as 'logical' thinking. Associated with this is the idea of 'inspiration' which in simple terms is a sudden realisation of a new way to categorise or separate 'facts' or 'knowledge'. What this means in practise is that one is able to look at what one has learned with a fresh perspective. Knowledge is best separated into categories that allow them to be easily pieced together in new and exciting ways. In this way Space and Time, or Air and Water, interact with one another in our Knowledge and Understanding to create the vibrant thunderstorms and lightning flashes of our consciousness.

Enchantment

The magical operation associated with the Wand of Air is that of enchantment. This is simply causing to manifest the magicians will, utilising some form of spell or ritual. Commonly used in Chaos Magic are sigils, of the kind popularised by Austin Osman Spare, where the letters in the statement of intent, repeated letters having been removed, are combined into some form of glyph. This is one technique that can be used and is exceedingly useful as a result of its simplicity.

Another popular technique is the practise of Sorcery, where physical objects are symbolically manipulated to represent the will of the magician. Such techniques are particularly grounding and help the magician escape from the distracting intellectual magical theories found in most books on the subject, probably including this one. Indeed I fully intend to ground my magic with a serious period of sorcery after I have finished writing this book, or maybe even before I have finished.

Enchantments are most often concerned with 'results magick', that is magick that has a real, definite and verifiable 'result', success or failure, as its outcome. If your magick is 'to become more spiritually enlightened' then it is very easy to kid yourself into believing you have succeeded, and too much of this can quickly lead to a magician suffering from what Phil Hine calls 'Magusitus'. Results magick can quickly tell you your magickal strengths and weaknesses and help curb feelings of immanent 'guru-hood'.

Air Elementals

The most common elementals of Air are known as sylphs, and are often depicted as the archetypal fairies with pretty faces, slender bodies and brightly coloured butterfly-like wings. Mythology, fiction and imagination can provide many more examples. It can be easy to anthropomorphise things like hurricanes and tornadoes, indeed meteorologists already give human names to hurricanes. The four winds are other examples, as are draughty places in your home may cause doors to open or close or swing to and fro as if the home were haunted. When next someone says 'its just the wind', think about this as meaning 'its just an Air Elemental'. Because of the association of Air with Space, it can be tempting to look at extra-terrestrial sightings as being related to Air Elementals. Space Elementals might be an apt description of many such sightings, where the beings seem to behave in a mischievous and whimsical way typical of what we would expect of an air elemental.

Another air related spirit worthy of attention, is the Chaos Butterfly, the flapping of whose wings can dramatically change the weather patterns on the other side of the planet. This butterfly can effectively be used to set in motion the storms of consciousness to take your ideas and awareness to previously unimagined and unexpected new 'tunnel-realities' and interpretations of experience. This can be extremely useful when one has entered a period where no new ideas seem to be challenging the way you think. If no new ideas seem forthcoming from without, why not conjure them up from within? A Chaos Butterfly will only be too pleased to help out in such a situation.

Water *(Time)* - Attraction Magic

There is no such thing as time,
particularly in Tanelorn,
particularly at the Conjunction of the Million Spheres.
Michael Moorcock

Attraction Magic is concerned with bringing things together, although it does not automatically involve any kind of union. The magicks of loving or consuming union can be found under descriptions of Love Magick, and War Magick respectively, in chapter 5. Ideas are brought together to form understandings of the way things are inter-related. This can happen intuitively or we can reach conscious understandings that we are able to put into words. Without this understanding our intelligence has a tendency towards cold facts which end up being applied without any understanding or concern for their wider consequences. This tunnel-vision is the biggest dilemma facing commercial science, whose rational ideology appears to be repeatedly failing the population at large, whilst mainstream scientists and sceptics repeatedly chant slogans like Occam's Razor as if they are some kind of unquestionable dogma or 'truth'. The New Age movement is full of crass commercialism, watered down misinterpretations of world beliefs, medieval attitudes and exploitative gurus, but on the whole poses no real threat to the world, other than problems of ignorance and apathy, which are manifestly worse in the general population, and on the other hand scientists continue to develop genetically modified foods which would appear to offer no benefits to anyone except the profits of a few big multinational biotech companies and supermarkets, more and more devices that increasingly demand an increase in the electrical power supply and mostly ignore the real problems of reducing our power needs and finding sustainable solutions to these problems.

Scientists then prefer to ignore their own faults whilst wildly criticising the New Age movement[29] for being 'irrational'. Is that 'rational' behaviour then?

Looked at in that way, 'rational' behaviour would appear to be quite idiotic, although in reality it is simply how we tend to behave when we lose touch with our understanding and interconnectedness. Unfortunately most of our scientific educational establishments are designed to select those who have a high tendency towards rational logic and tend to be off putting to those with a broader understanding. It would seem that science is in desperate need of a different kind of intellect, but it isn't going to get it unless it changes the whole way science is taught in the first place.

And so it seems that it is up to the individual to try to gain an understanding of what the implications and consequences of various new technologies will be. Robert Anton Wilson has promoted the idea of being Homo Neophilus, but we mustn't make the mistake of accepting everything new simply because it is new. Most new technologies will probably have a use that is beneficial to humankind and to nature, but will be exploited for profit in ways which do more harm than good, by companies that couldn't care less about anything other than their shareholders' abstract economic 'gain' (which amounts to little more than bigger numbers on a balance sheet, and not actually anything of any benefit to anyone).

In such a climate many are tempted to halt, or reverse, the process of individualisation and globalisation and return to nationalist 'nation-state' type power structures. Such socialism and/or fascism tends towards a great decrease in personal freedom and attempting to solve environmental problems through

---

[29]*However much it could do with the criticism is besides the point, New Agers are hardly likely to take any notice of a scientist.*

high 'eco-taxes', without implementing any real lasting solutions. Such nations would quickly become isolated and decline into poverty, without actually having achieved anything to benefit the environment.

In such a climate of global individualism, it is up to the people to realise where the power now lies and to choose carefully which companies they wish to support. Consumerism is the new politics. When you buy something, anything, you are not just buying a product any more, you are having your say in how the world is run. Actual democratic government is quickly becoming an obsolete force with only limited power. Rule by money may seem unfairly balanced towards the rich, but one of the choices facing us is whether we are prepared to pay more for products that contribute towards creating a climate that pays better wages. Are we prepared to boycott companies that underpay their staff or exploit third-world workers? It is not for me to tell you how to spend, each individual needs to work out their own policy on the matter. But we will only see true 'consumer democracy' emerge when the public are given full information about what it is they are buying and who they are buying it from. This perhaps is the role democratic government should be playing, making sure such information is easily available to the consumer, a role they are not currently performing very well. Magic to aid the spread of understanding of these and other important issues is mostly a part of this kind of magic. Those with a direct link to wealth and the environment may well have connections with resources, and issues such as sustainability.

At the other extreme, attraction magic is magic whose purpose is to draw two things together, or attract something to a certain place, such as punters to a musical performance or magical conference. You may be organising an event you wish a certain famous speaker to attend and give a speech, or you may just wish to attract a high quality of speakers and/or performers. You may just wish to attract some customers into your place of commerce. You may have set up a bird-watching trip and wish to attract some interesting species, or maybe meditating in a forest and wish to attract a totem animal spirit to make itself known to you. Or it might be that you are searching for a particular object, even if you are not quite sure what it is, and you just wish to 'draw' it to you, or make 'yourself' attracted to 'it'. All of these examples can be achieved with simple attraction magic spells.

Divination

The magical operation associated with the cup, the magical weapon of water, is the art of divination, which is to say the art of seeing events, happenings and possibilities in far off parts of space-time. A discussion of some specific divination techniques relevant to the Kaosphere will be discussed in Appendix D, whilst here we will discuss theories on the mechanics of divination in general. One may consider that this technique involves quantum teleporting, that is to say that the strange entanglements that can occur between particles seemingly some distance away from one another.

One may prefer to see it as observing the connection between seemingly separate aspects of the space-time fractal, and how changes in one reflect changes in the other. Changes in one part of the space-time fractal and another part may be indicative of a fluctuation at the seed level. Current physical theories are beginning to point to the possibility that our universe, our space-time dimensions, our waves and particles, the laws of both quantum mechanics and general relativity, manifest out of a random noise of chaotic information, beyond space and time. If the universe exhibits a fractal quality, and it would seem that it does, then the random noise will dramatically effect how the various patterns in space-time-energy-mass emerge, and since fractal patterns exhibit self-similarity on various scales and locations on the fractal, then it is possible to read general trends from one pattern to a pattern that will emerge, is emerging or has emerged in local parts of the space-time continuum. The less local the two patterns being compared, the more distortion will occur between them[30].

---

[30]*This is the significance of the butterfly effect, a tiny deviation will make little difference on the short term, but over the long term will manifest in a huge deviation. This causes self-similarity to be greatly distorted in remote parts of a fractal, to*

Mostly however, it is best to simply practise the art and try to understand what is happening without using words. Which is not the same as saying that one shouldn't study the theory behind the system you are using. For example, if you are using Tarot, then the images and symbols of each card should be well understood, perhaps on several levels simultaneously, and the cosmological map that is used to lay the cards out should also be familiar to the reader, with every significance and inter-relation of the map well understood. This may not be the case in the early stages of using a new unfamiliar divination system, during which time the reader is endeavouring to learn the system, practise being one of the ways in which a new system can be learned.

Water, or time is not concerned with logic and reason, as might be air, but with understanding. Its purpose is to give the reader an understanding of the subject, by which is meant forming connections between the subject and the meanings of various symbols. The theory is that this can lead to deeper understandings of the subject. The reader may choose one of any number of things to be the subject in any particular reading, including themselves, someone else, a particular problem or concern, a delicate political situation, a pet, knowledge of how to approach a particular spell, enchantment, invocation or evocation, the performance of a servitor, the advantages of buying a particular object, what to do at the weekend or what influence on my life will 'so-and-so' have.

One danger to beware of in a divination is 'self-fulfilling prophecy'. Having divined something, and with enough belief in what one has read, it can be all too easy to turn a divination into an enchantment[31]. When the divination has shown a desirable outcome this is rarely a problem, but can be disastrous if the divination has shown an undesirable outcome. An experienced magician will no doubt be aware of this potentiality and will be able to use enchantment and other methods to redress the undesirable situation. When performing readings for people

---

the extent that the patterns become unrecognisable.
[31] *Hence showing how space and time aren't quite as separate as the illusion of existence leads us to believe.*

unversed in magickal knowledge, especially those prone to absolute belief in what you are telling them, it is generally not a good idea to hide from them anything negative you may have seen, however much you may be tempted to do so in order to prevent self-fulfilling prophecy. This is because the subconscious mind of the person you are reading for will pick up on the subliminal signals you resultantly emit. Instead it is better to be up front with them about the problem but offer to correct the situation magically or make it clear that this future is not predetermined and tell them that they are always in control of their own destiny.

There would be little point performing divination in a deterministic universe, since you would be able to change nothing, instead the purpose of divination is to try to work out where unseen dangers may be hidden, so that they may be avoided.

Another method of divination is that of scrying, where the object is to gain hallucinatory experiences and to use the patterns thus seen to predict other patterns within the fractal. Perhaps the most accessible and well known of this type of divination is dream interpretation. We all frequently hallucinate during dream sleep, and such hallucinations are often very powerful and vivid. They totally immerse the awareness so that one is not even aware that one is hallucinating. The trick is to remember them upon waking and to record them. In practise this is best not done whilst fully awake, but performed continually throughout the morning every time wakefulness begins to appear, followed by sinking back into a new dream. In this way many dreams a night may be recorded, and meanings taken from the patterns each describe.

In lucid dream the magician is in control of the dream and so symbols may not contain divinatory meaning, however if the magician is crafty, they may 'create' a scrying bowl or tarot deck within the dream that they may use with ease. The magician is likely to gain very vivid hallucinations in a dream created scrying bowl, much more easily than might be obtained in wakefulness, but may combine the advantage of deliberate purpose that asking a question to a scrying bowl provides. In this way one isn't left wondering whether the dream meant something or not. The trick is to remember what question you intended to ask whilst in the dream, or to sigilise it before sleep and be lucid that there was a question even if one can't remember it.

The use of scrying bowls, crystal balls and black mirrors is another hallucinatory method that is commonly used for divinatory purposes. With practise the magician may enter dreamlike states of 'vacuity' where images simply appear in the awareness and can be recorded. As with dreams the magician must leave this mind state in order to put into words what has been seen.

Perhaps one of the most obvious methods of obtaining a hallucinatory experience is via the consumption of substances known to induce that very effect, although not always a legal course of action in many parts of the world. Indeed, there is much evidence to suggest that the caves where many of the oracles used to practise their arts had natural fissures that gave off hallucinatory gasses. Shamans the world over always know where to find various fungi, cacti, herbs and/or animal secretions that have this kind of effect, although this kind of experience can have many more uses for a magician than simple divination. Perhaps in most cases this would be a too extreme method since the divination may be over long before the magician recovers from the effects.

Although mind altering substances can be used in magic to great effect, any magician that wishes to use them successfully would have to be well practised in the magickal arts whilst sober in order to gain any real benefit from the experience. In all cases the taking of substances should be at the discretion of the individual and there are equally good magicians who take them as don't take them, and many who only do so on the odd occasion.

Water Elementals

Spirits of water are most commonly known as undines, and shown to be like mermaids or mer-people with the head, arms and upper torso of a human, but with the tail of a fish. Related to these water spirits are the Norse seal-girls. However, like the spirits of other elements, not all spirits of water sit comfortably with such images. Although it may seem 'new-age' to mention them, the popular images of a dolphin as a watery intelligence shouldn't necessarily be overlooked as a potential image for water spirits.

The mythologies of the world contain many sea monsters, sea serpents and dragons from the depths, and these represent a much more powerful, uncontrollable and perhaps even destructive side to water. Depending on your need, these can be of assistance in some water magick, but may prove crude and lacking in precision.

Octopus, Squid, Cuttlefish, Crabs and Lobsters have a sinister appeal, and can be related to the fiction of H.P.Lovecraft and creatures of Cthulu. Indeed many magicians have worked with Cthulu, and the author has had some interesting results from working with a Cthulu-like deity in dream work. Experiences with Cthulu needn't take on a sinister nature, although if you fear, want or expect it to, then it probably will. My own experiences have proved awesome in nature, but not terror inducing, and the deity concerned, once I had found him, was fairly communicative and co-operative. The Cthulu of Lovecraft's stories has obvious dream connections, and so spirits of this nature can undoubtedly be used to effect in dreamwork. Other forms of hallucinatory experience, such as pathworkings, have also proved popular with this paradigm.

Amphibian creatures also have water connections, and it isn't too surprising to learn that some species of toad give off bodily secretions that can induce hallucinatory experiences. A particular gland in such toads, strong in the hallucinatory substance, is thought to be, in some contexts, what the alchemist's meant by the philosopher's stone. Once removed from the toad, the gland looks like a stone. This is possibly an explanation of why witches were often associated with toads, and the ability to turn people into toads may well have come from the witch tricking the subject into imbibing toad secretions and then suggesting to them that they were now a toad at the moment of imprint vulnerability. This might not always have been malicious, since it may well have been the opening part of an otherwise quite beneficial transformative process. Of course, there is no doubt it could be used for harm, and probably would have been, and even a satisfied client who had undergone such a transformation would thereafter think doubly twice about crossing the witch, and may well have believed that the witch really had turned them into a toad. Of course, in a magickal sense they really would have been.

Folklore, traditional tales and mythology from around the world reveal many other water creatures which may be of use in such situations, such as the salmon of wisdom, sirens and water-nymphs. One doesn't have to look far to find references. It can be equally rewarding to construct your own water spirits. Imagining a person made entirely of water is helped by images of water elementals found in popular role-playing games and fantasy trading card games such as Magic the Gathering and water related creatures found in Pokemon. Toys and games contain powerful imagery that speaks to us on a level we were at in early development and can thus pull triggers in our consciousness that can operate an innocent, amoral and experimental side of us that is willing to believe in anything that offers us fun. If we allow that doorway to be opened then we can gain access to some powerful magick.

5. The Eight Colours of Magic

Every cult has to have its logo. Thelema has the unicursal hexagram, witchcraft has the pentagram, satanism has the goat's head, P.T.V. had the psychic cross, Masonry has its 'divide and rule', and Chaos magic has the eight rayed 'star of Chaos'. This is eight arrows emanating from a black circle, supposedly having its origins in ancient Babylon. Such a cuniform does exist, or at least something vaguely like it, representing the force of 'divinity'.

Dr Nathan Satan[32]

The 'Eight Colours of Magic' system of Carroll was based on the symbol known as the Chaosphere which under the name of 'The Sigil of Chaos' has its origins in the fiction of Moorcock. Since its inception at the hands of Moorcock the symbol has become immensely popular in a diverse range of subcultures, including the role-playing games of 'Dungeons and Dragons' and 'Warhammer', the comic 2000AD, Chaos Current Punks, certain Thrash Metal bands, a few branches of Techno music, various fantasy artists and not to mention the Chaos Magic movement itself.

Alchemically speaking, the symbol is highly unbalanced. At its centre is a circle, which could represent the element of Earth. From this are eight outwards pointing arrows, which could represent the element of Fire. From this standpoint the symbol seems to say 'Earth Inferno'. The illustrations that begin each chapter of this book present more balanced variants, as does the 'Kaos Hieroglyph' itself.

However, there is a pleasing symmetry to the Chaosphere and a powerful simplicity. None of the alternatives presented in this book are intended to replace the Chaosphere. Especially as an exoteric symbol, the Chaosphere works best as it is.

Either way the symbols hint at a magic system based on the

---

32 Dr Nathan Satan, *"Liber Pariah"*, (Norwich, 2001).

number eight. Carroll based his on planetary symbols and Crowley's Qabala. Both have their roots in medieval alchemy. The serious student of these mysteries will research these sources for themselves. Another system of eight's also worthy of inspection is Leary's 'Eight Circuits'. For older systems look to the I-Ching, the nine worlds of the Celtic mysteries and the nine worlds of the Norse mysteries. Systems of eight are related to systems of nine in the same way systems of four are related to systems of five and dualistic systems are related to systems of threes. Three, Five and Nine represent the combining of their own level of duality with the transcendent source of Mercury, the Tao, Aether, Quintessence, Kia or Chi.

White Magic
The characteristics of the neuroelectric circuit are high velocity, multiple choice, relativity, and the fission-fusion of all perceptions into parallel science-fiction universes of alternate possibilities.
Robert Anton Wilson

Psyche Magic is the magic of the inner-self-being. The superficial opposite of Psyche Magic is Ego Magick, magic of the outer-self-being. White magic is an entirely new concept, not present in Carroll's chaosphere system and only introduced in my Cybermorphic Kaosphere System[33].

Like Yellow Magic, Psyche Magic seems to express itself in

---

[33] *See chapter 1. This type of magic is not really new, most magical practitioners will recognise this type of magic as mysticism and/or psychology. Much of the magic already performed by chaos magicians will find a happy home in this category. Some of this may have previously escaped categorisation, or may have been uneasily slotted into 'Yellow Magic'. I hope that by providing this new system I am offering a much needed new category, more consistent with our actual experience of magic and of life.*

combination with the other colours. Pure White magic is the magic of the totally internal self, all the aspects of oneself that one never reveals, except perhaps at some therapy session or with a friend that you trust utterly but more likely never reveal even to yourself. White-Yellow magic is magic with all the suppressed identities that you've never had the courage to show the world, such as the closet transvestite, who only dresses up for his own pleasure, never revealing his secret inner identity to anyone, or the teenager who secretly pretends to be a rock star. White-Black concerns all our most morbid inner thoughts and fears concerning our mortality. White-Red concerns all our repressed hatred and aggression. White-Orange concerns all our unresolved stress and fear. White-Blue concerns all our secret desires and pleasure drives, our wildest fantasies. White-Green concerns all our suppressed passions and love. White-Purple our inner creative drive, our inner muse. All magic on the inner self concerns reprogramming various parts of our mind. Psyche Magic can be seen to correlate to circuit VI, the meta-programming circuit, in Timothy Leary's eight circuit model of the mind.

Psyche Magic Ritual

An example of a white magic ritual is the following Child Abuse Ritual, where an adult who suffered abuse as a child, in the form of rape and torture can be healed of the worst psychological effects. These psychological effects are usually caused by a demon that is summoned by the abuser and placed into the victim's mind during the abuse. Children are particularly magically vulnerable anyway, and the gnosis of shear terror is enough to cause the creation of an extremely powerful demon. The abuser tells the victim that if they should ever tell anyone about the abuse then s/he will come and kill everyone in the room and then slowly torture the victim to death.

The child, in a state of absolute terror believes this and for the sake of its own survival decides to go along with this idea. The child is psychically manipulated to create a demon within their own head which ever reminds them that they will be killed and tortured if they should ever reveal what had happened. If the abuse has stopped, then the child will suppress this demon, but it will still lurk there in the deepest part of the mind, usually resurfacing during adolescence when the child remembers what happened to them. A psychically aware child may accidentally create further demons to protect themselves from the original one.

Such demons are usually very easy to deal with as they were created by the victim themselves and so generally have very little ill intent towards the victim, in fact their mission is to protect their creator from the original demon. They can be scary, and have been known to cause poltergeist activity. They can be easily dealt with using a simple banishing, best performed with the consent of the victim or by the victim themselves if at all possible.

After the outer demons have been banished, the main demon still lurks and continues to cause problems throughout the victim's life. This demon also is more destructive since it was programmed by the abuser and has only the intent of the abuser as its main goal. It will attempt to destroy the victim's life and will use the victims own actions, which it partly controls from within, to ensure all the victim's relationships fail, or some equally negative suggestion, planted during the abuse by the abuser. It has a parasitic or vampiric relationship with the victim, and although it lives in the victim's mind and partly controls the victims actions, it should be properly viewed as a separate entity. If the victim can be taught to view this demon as a separate entity from themselves then they have effectively prepared themselves for the following ritual which will rid themselves of the demon for good.

In between the victim realising that the demon is a separate parasitic entity, which can be permanently removed, and the time of the actual rite to remove the demon, is a time fraught with danger. The demon could try and dissuade the victim from taking part, could try and urge the victim into violence or could try causing poltergeist activity. All these things and other possible symptoms should be watched out for, and the rite should be performed as quickly as possible.

Preparation:

① The demon should be described in a sentence, such as 'Dark robed figure from the boy of torture and rape'

② The description should be turned into a demonic name, which can be done by listing all the letters which appear in the description an odd number of times. Vowels can be repeated if needed to make the name pronounceable. The phrase above revealed the name Krigmoth Pandefy.

③ A sigil should be made from the letters in this name.

④ A sigil of protection should be made from a phrase such as 'This sigil protects the wearer from, and gives them power over, the foul demon Krigmoth Pandefy'

⑤ An image of the demon, such as a sketch or symbolic biscuit, should be made and etched with the demons sigil.

⑥ Anything required to destroy the image, such as a candle and ash-tray for burning it or a pestle and mortar for crushing it into oblivion, should be obtained.

⑦ The participants may wish to bath or shower before the rite to help them mentally prepare. (Optional)

After this preparation is completed, the ritual is ready to be performed. The image and all equipment should be somewhere inside the ritual area. The following steps should be followed.

Ritual

❶ Everyone should draw the sigil of protection on their foreheads.

❷ A magician performs some form of banishing to create a sealed space. This should seal all escape routes of the demon so that once summoned, it will be trapped in the ritual area. The four cardinal directions plus up and down should be sufficient.

❸ A magician leads the statement of intent, such as 'It is our will to destroy the demon Krigmoth Pandefy'.

❹ All magicians command Krigmoth Pandefy to become present whilst the patient silently projects it outwards from inside of them.

❺ When the demon has appeared, Everyone commands the demon into the image and seals it inside the image so that it cannot escape. Once it is inside, a phrase such as 'I magically seal you in this image so that you may never escape from it.' or 'I command you, Krigmoth Pandefy, to become one with this image, so that the life of this image becomes your life, its death, your death.' should suffice.

❻ The patient destroys the image using their chosen means. If the patient is unable to do so, they may signal for another magician to destroy it on their behalf. It is important that the magician obtains the patient's permission to do so if this happens.

❼ The patient makes a statement concerning what they intend to do with the part of their mind they have just freed from the tyranny of the demon. Such a declaration prevents the new space from being easily occupied by anything the patient doesn't want. A vacuum is always filled.

❽ Space for all to reflect, and to make sure nothing else needs to be done.

❾ The magician that sealed the ritual area removes the seals, effectively ending the rite.

This is the most effective way I am aware of for healing the kind of mental damage caused by the torture and abuse of a child. One must be careful to realise that the patient will probably still have various behavioural abnormalities which they will need to adjust for themselves, the ritual will not free them of all psychological imbalance and neurosis. Rather it is a highly specialised surgery to remove a very specific neurosis. The technique has many more uses. Any kind of destructive habit pattern, either implanted or suggested from an outside source, or developed oneself, can be treated as a demon if you want it removed. The technique of evocation/exorcism is intense but powerfully effective. It can be used to treat the psychological effects of adult rape, drug addictions such as heroin, alcohol and tobacco, or annoying habits such as bum-scratching, nail biting or nose-picking.

Some of these examples may seem trivial compared to the others, but as far as the technique is concerned the size of the demon is relatively unimportant. What matters is that you were able to detach yourself from it and identify it as a separate entity that had begun acting as a parasite on yourself.

Yellow Magic

> Our sense of being an individual emerges from clusters of beliefs, attitudes, self-definitions, inner conversations, boundaries and projections of 'otherness'. We move each day through a highly complex field of social relations, assuming roles, wearing carefully-crafted masks, and tacitly agreeing to play by the rules of Consensus, or Paramount Reality.
>
> Phil Hine[34]

Ego magic is the magic of glamours. We all use them, even if it seems we are 'unglamorous'. An image is an image, and the appearance of not being glamorous can have its own power, although often it is not as fun. At the same time it is not always fun to be continuously the centre of attention and so a glamour of ordinariness has its uses.

Our glamours are our masks. The wise magician has an

---

34 Phil Hine, *'Condensed Chaos: An Introduction to Chaos Magic'*, (Tempe, AZ, 1995), p.125

array of masks suitable for every occasion, some for fun, some for work, some for magic. Some to be noticed, some to hide behind, some to blend in. Some to look poor, others to look rich. The key is to project the image of yourself you want to project in any circumstances. This magic is most effective if you can do it on the spot, just when you need it. However, this isn't to say that formal ritual can't be of use. Suppose you want to put across a side of yourself you haven't been in tune with of late. First put on the appropriate clothes and look at your image in the mirror. Get it right. Then use ritual method to bring into your consciousness the qualities you desire to put across. When you have succeeded with this you are ready to take that personality out into the outside world.

One method I have found of particular use, is to do this over a long period of time in the comfort of your own home before revealing the new self to the public. Build up your confidence and association with the new persona before subjecting it to the eyes of others. Then when you do go public with it, you will have already developed the character of your persona to some extent, and ironed out some of the unwanted flaws.

Ego magic relates to Circuit II in Leary's model, the Emotional-Territorial circuit. In this sense it relates to how well we create our personal space and boundaries, and our abilities to dominate and submit when the occasion demands it. In our lives we associate with many different social circles and occupy differing roles and levels of respect in each. In some we may be looked on as a leader, an elder and/or an authority. In another group simultaneously we may be considered a peer, an equal among friends and share in a mutual respect. Whilst in another group you may be in a position of subservience, inexperience or without responsibility. In all these social circles we occupy the space we fall or grow into. Few of us really desire to be dominant in all our societies. It would place too much responsibility and pressure upon us. Such a misguided desire in magical groups is what leads to 'magusitus' and a similar power-hunger leads to parallel imbalances in other walks of life.

A much more desirable state of affairs is to have the freedom to submit and have a place in which to do that. In that place we can be free of all responsibility, let others take control while we just enjoy the ride. This is why fairground rides are popular, and why stressed out businessmen pay out large sums of money to be tied up, beaten and humiliated. It is why it is fun to relax and watch a play or performance on stage. Or even to just watch a film, at home or at the cinema.

We all need friends who are peers. It is, as they say, lonely at the top. But it can also be equally lonely at the bottom. Among equals you can share similar concerns, ideas and feel the warmth of mutual understanding. Trying to dominate or submit to your peer group would be out of place behaviour and would likely lose you the respect of the group concerned. It may even lose you the ability to go somewhere where you can be equals with others.

Having recognised places were it is important to relate to others as peers, and where it is well to submit, one may achieve greater ability to take control and lead when that is asked of you. Leadership is not so much a fixed status of superiority over others as it is a responsibility to take control for a while and make sure you don't screw things up, whilst everyone else relaxes and leaves the thinking up to you.

In a magical group where everyone gets a chance to lead a ritual in an intense weekend of workings, the person leading the ritual is temporarily 'the leader' whilst everyone who takes part in the ritual is for a short time subservient. For the duration of the ritual the leader directs and controls everyone else to achieve the desired results (hopefully). Everyone else takes part, and puts effort in, but they just perform as directed. Come the interludes between rituals people relate as peers, during the 'official' business of the group, some kind of official or unspoken hierarchy or power structure will likely become more apparent. Then as someone else starts the next ritual, they become for a time a new leader, and the leader of the previous ritual can enjoy a more relaxed subservient role.

If you cannot submit, you cannot lead. If you cannot be superior and inferior when you need to, how can you be equal? Dominance, equality and submission are all just tools for the creation of masks. Uniforms, robes, street clothes or nudity don't make any difference. This circuit is always there, as are all the

108

others. All the techniques of uniform, robes and going skyclad achieve in ritual is to present a different kind of mask, a mask of conformity. We are all in this uniform. We are all in this robe. We are all naked. Even doing rituals in street clothes says 'we are all the same because we are all in our normal clothes'. We are all the same because we are all individuals...

Blue Magic

The Chaos approach stresses that fun and pleasure are important, yet often neglected dimensions of magic. Can magic be entertaining? Play and entertainment tend to be undervalued, yet they are arguably two of the most significant of human experiences, and magic and play share common features. Both are defined in contrast to the everyday world. Both serve to draw the participant out from the ordinary world into the mythic, larger-than-life dimension. What is the difference between a child playing with a doll and an 'adult' sorcerer enchanting over a wax image?
Phil Hine[35]

Play magic is the magic of using/spending other beings for our own ends. These 'other beings' can include physical objects such as toys, games, food, clothes and other things that make our lives pleasurable and more beautiful, and also more intangible things such as time, money, intelligence and our skills and abilities. Play is about how effectively we use our resources for our pleasure and leisure. Play magic is about using magic to enhance our possibilities for experiencing pleasure and leisure activities and for reaching increasingly heightened and intensified states of pleasure consciousness.

---

35 Phil Hine, *'Condensed Chaos: An Introduction to Chaos Magic'*, (Tempe, AZ, 1995), pp. 88-89.

To fully realise your potential for pleasure one must first discover ones own dreams, for if you haven't fully recognised what gives you pleasure, then you can end up wasting much time and resources pursuing other people's fantasies. In the modern age more people have the wealth, freedom and potential to experience many more diverse forms of pleasure than ever before, as has been the general trend of humanity since the dawn of pre-history to slowly increase the time and resources for leisure and pleasure.

At the same time the resultant boom of consumerism has lead to a bombardment of media images promoting diverse forms of leisure and pleasure activities, which may or may not be what you seek to spend your life enjoying. Distracted from your true desires, persuaded that they aren't normal, or even that they aren't pleasurable, it can become possible to waste a huge portion of your life chasing bland consumerist visions of other people's desires.

With so much choice, we are faced with making the decision of what is pleasurable for us. A lot of this introspection may involve a combination of white and blue magic. Get to experience a wide variety of different pleasures, whilst using inner reflection to weed out those that don't really do it for you. Most things are enjoyable once, but only the things that really turn you on are worth repeating more than a couple of times. Be honest with yourself, don't do something you know you won't enjoy, just because all your friends are doing it. Play Magic can be seen to correlate to circuit V, the neuro-somatic circuit, in Timothy Leary's eight circuit model of the mind.

It is thought that humanity in general is moving out of Circuit IV consciousness (The Sexual-Morality Circuit, The Aeon of Bureaucracy/Atheism) and into Circuit V consciousness (The Pleasure Circuit, The Aeon of Aftermath/Chaoism). This means that essentially the centre of power is moving away from organisations that dictate moral/law structures (religions and governments), and towards organisations that provide us with leisure and pleasure goods and activities (multi-national corporations, especially media, music, film and food). When people begin to realise the rate at which this power exchange is taking place and what it essentially means, they will demand more

110

democratic control. The only way they can do this is by boycotting the goods of those companies that behave in ways we don't like and supporting those that behave in ways we do. Like it or not, we are living in an age of 'one penny, one vote'. It is time we exercised control over what we spend that on. Of course it is not for me to tell you how to use your control, this only something you can do yourself. I only suggest that individuals look at the ways in which they spend their resources shapes the world we live in.

Another trend is the massive upsurge in interest in all things fetish and bondage related. Kinky is in. This is reflected in the moves away from the bland, frumpy, prudery that dictated forth aeon fashion, towards the more exotic and daring fashions currently gaining in rapid popularity in the fetish scene. Not that all fashion in the fifth aeon will be based around leather, pvc and rubber! I expect that more conventional materials will also be used in ways that excite and tempt. Again, individual taste will become an important factor, but expect that many people will diversify those tastes rather than being stuck in the same fashion paradigms all the time. A wide wardrobe of diverse costumes can also be important in yellow magic, and the image of fun we present to others is an area of yellow-blue overlap.

Play Magic Ritual

A Play Magic ritual I recently performed involved the creation of a Play Magic servitor. To fit the theme I bought a child's doll from a charity shop and painted it blue. The symbolism here should be obvious. A doll is a toy, something to play with and the doll I chose was bought second hand, meaning it had already been played with. Blue is the colour of play magic, and on top of this I painted gold automatic sigils.

The idea of the ritual is to get everyone into a regressed state of consciousness, so that we all become as children again. The idea is that, as children our subconscious minds are much more accessible, and much less subject to the interference of the conscious mind.

Remember, it is better to let the following ritual description inspire your own ideas than it is to copy it exact. Magic is better aided by originality and creativity than it is dogmatic adherence to a supposedly correct 'formula'. The only reason for my listing these rituals in this book is so that the beginner may gain some understanding of ritual structure and technique, better enabling them to construct their own ideas. Also so that experienced magicians may gain inspiration from techniques and structure they may not have tried.

Preparation:

① The blue magic servitor should be prepared according to your inspiration.

② A name should be sought for the servitor using whatever method pleases you. I personally wrote a phrase describing the dolls purpose and deleted all letters appearing an even number of times. Re-arranging the remaining letters revealed the name Kazeebo.

③ A rhyme should be made around this name, preferably based on a nursery rhyme. The rhyme I used was...

Sing a song of pleasure
A Blue Doll full o' treasure
Kazeebo
Kazeebo
We all have fun!

④ Enough toys for all included in the rite need to be at hand.

⑤ Arrange the servitor in the centre of the ritual space with all the toys.

Ritual
❶ The ritual space is prepared using a suitable banishing rite.

❷ All present become as children, regressing to the age of a child between 5 and 10. In a large group it may be useful to have one magician remain at least partially as an adult.

❸ All 'children' play with their toys, putting their wish for a pleasure sought into the toys as they do so.

❹ At a suitable point all stop and a statement of intent is spoken aloud. The first time round this will be something like 'It is our Will to create Kazeebo, a blue magic servitor, so that she may grant us our desires for pleasure'. Later evocations will be more along the lines of 'It is our Will to evoke Kazeebo, so that she may grant us our wishes for pleasure.'

❺ The rhyme is repeated by all five times. In the case of the above rhyme, which was based on 'ring a ring o' roses', this is accompanied by joining hands and dancing round in a circle, falling down and pointing at the servitor on the last 'fun'. In this rite, banishment by laughter is most appropriate, since the whole idea is fun, pleasure and enjoyment. It should come quite naturally at this point.

There are many ways to do Play Magic rituals, and not all need involve the innocence of childhood. Adults play at many games, and many of these may not be suitable for children. These games too may be included into a Play Magic ritual. There are many other activities that involve pleasure and fun, such as dancing, music, watching fireworks, surfing, skateboarding, skiing and swimming.

All of these things can be fun. If you find something fun and think you can incorporate it into a Play Magic rite, then try it. If you have fun doing the magic, you are more likely to gain the fun of your wish. This is a basic sympathetic magic principle, like attracts like, you get out of magic what you put in.

Orange Magic

Always you have been told that work is a
curse and labour a misfortune.
But I say to you that when you work you
fulfil a part of earth's furthest dream,
assigned to you when that dream was born,
And in keeping yourself with labour you are
in truth loving life,
And to love life through labour is to be
intimate with life's inmost secret.
Kahlil Gibran[36]

Work is magic concerned with the acquisition, collection and organisation of resources. We all need to work in order to have the resources we need to enjoy life, in order to increase our potential for play. The history of humanity has been a gradual process of making work more efficient, so we can spend less time and effort in actual labour and more time in enjoying the fruits of our labour. In the recent history (of the last few thousand years) certain groups of human society began to decrease the amount of work they did by increasing the amount of work other humans

---

36 Kahlil Gibran, *'The Prophet'* (St Ives, UK, 1992), pp. 35-36.

had to do. Even more recently religion has made work a 'sacred duty', and the avoidance of work has been labelled 'laziness' and a 'sin'. Therefore a large portion of the worlds population are spending more time working than is actually economically necessary. This unfortunately has a knock on effect on prices, making things more expensive than they need to be. If the whole world worked part-time then everything would still get done, and prices would even out to affordable levels. The other problem is guilt. Rather than enjoy their free time, a great many people are wasting it by vegetating mindlessly in front of a television, even when there is nothing on that they really want to watch. Others commute on two-hour each way journeys to work, meaning a huge chunk of their life experience is tied up in driving their car or taking train journeys.

Work Magic is related to Leary's Circuit III, the semantic, time binding circuit. This circuit it related to the concept of using language to pass down ideas from generation to generation, the building of tools, and the communication and development of ideas, especially the cumulative effect of these ideas to create new ideas. The Circuit III ideas provide a bridge between the seemingly different concepts of Work Magic and Carroll's Thinking Magic. The accumulation of ideas and knowledge is easily correlated to thinking. But the development of ideas are fuelled by work. The skilled professions became the knowledge bases of various skills, techniques and ideas, which in many cases resulted in closely guarded trade secrets. Even the 'Great Work' of alchemy fits this pattern. In as much as new ideas have a knock on effect on the stability of political and religious thinking, they are seen as dangerous to the political and religious authorities. Which probably goes some way to explaining why these two types of institution are perhaps slowest on the uptake of the New, and why they try to suppress them when given the opportunity. Thus the true goal of work, to increase the efficiency of our efforts to acquire the resources needed for survival and pleasure, has been subverted by the authorities into a 'sacred duty', a 'contribution to society' and all sorts of other self righteous nonsense.

Such ideas can lead to a bohemian rebellion and many magicians may find themselves unemployed and scraping a living from benefits, believing that because they are having fun it doesn't matter. Maybe it doesn't, but I have found that such a state of existence can lead to the lack of ability to do those things I really want to do. This is usually due to lack of ability to pay. To acquire any reasonable amount of money, some effort needs to be expended. It doesn't matter if you are begging on the streets, stealing or writing computer software, without effort you will get nowhere. Or more precisely you will earn nothing.

There is nothing cool about being on benefits. Its hard work filling out all those forms and persuading social services that you are really looking for work. Its hard work trying to live off a small amount of money, trying to balance a small budget so that you can eat enough to live and still have a little for a social life. I've been there and the only thing that can really be said for it is the amount of free time available. The only good thing about benefits is that they provide a safety net, something to fall on in times of need.

Full time work takes up far too much time, although it does have the benefit of bringing plenty of money into your life. One solution to this problem is to earn money doing something you enjoy and find fun. Most magicians have an inner sense of something they want to achieve in their life, and if money can be earned whilst pursuing this personal ambition, then it is well that it should be. Even then, the earning of money usually involves a certain amount of compromise and pandering to the tastes of those who do the paying. As such even full-time employment in something we enjoy can restrict our freedom. Short of a sudden windfall that means we never have to work again, the only practical answer for most of us is part-time employment. This can mean a lot of organisation in your life because it can be easy to become too dependant on the income brought in from a full time job. If however, you can earn enough money to live whilst only working part-time, and this can be eased if your partner also holds a part-time position, then you can reap the benefits of an increased wealth of time. When learning to run your own business they try to teach you that time = money. The Sufi's offer us a different perspective however. One of their stories contains the message that when it is your time to die, all the money in the world cannot buy you a single hour...

116

Black Magic

BLACK SWORD, BLACK SWORD, BLACK SWORD
THE BLADE OF THE SWORD
HAS THE BLOOD OF THE SUN
THE HILT OF THE SWORD
AND THE HAND ARE AS ONE
BLACK SWORD, BLACK SWORD, BLACK SWORD
AROUSE THE BLACK BLADE
AND THE PATTERN IS MADE
THE DEED WILL BE DONE
AND THE PRICE WILL BE PAID
BLACK SWORD, BLACK SWORD, BLACK SWORD
Michael Moorcock

Death is an area of magic that has a much maligned and negative image. In the west the colour black is associated with it, whereas in the east its colour is white. In this, the colours black and white can be seen to be interchangeable between death and psyche, for black is also the colour of the darkest abyss in our subconscious, in space or at the bottom of the ocean where Sun's ray's cannot penetrate. White is the colour of bone. In the Kaosphere system, Death Magic is the magic of entropy, negative dividing processes that destroy complexity and reduce them to their simplest components. Processes of decay.

It is the first half of the mystery of Thanateros, the clearing away of the old to make way for new growth. This is of course a cyclic mystery rather than a linear one with a definite beginning and end. Working with black magic allows us to release from our lives unwanted influences, forces and governing factors. We may have begun a habit, project or relationship that was once useful to us, but these things can outgrow their usefulness and become a nuisance. It may even be material possessions that you need to let go of. If you live in a small flat and have filled it to capacity with material belongings, to the extent you can now hardly move, then it is possibly time to clear out a load of stuff that you no longer need. Then again you may choose to bring to an end the era of

118

living somewhere so small. Perhaps you may even do both!

Releasing these things needn't be a waste, you may have a friend who needs some of it and would willingly take it off your hands. You may be able to sell some of it for cash. Or you may be able to donate it to a charity shop. There are always many options open, and such exercises of release can only be of benefit because your life will be enriched for the extra space you have gained yourself.

Harder than this is the clearing of space in your mind, the release of unwanted ideology, hang ups and bad memories. But any efforts in this area will reap far greater rewards, since if your mind is full of unwanted clutter, you will feel crowded no matter how much material space you have.

But there is a lot more to Black magic than simply release. Black magic corresponds to Circuit VII of Leary's system, the DNA consciousness circuit. This relates not only to our relationship with our own mortality and our quest for immortality, but also to our ancestral memories. In recent years the term ancestor has been applied only in a genetic sense. This has lead to a rather narrow racial view of ancestral tradition, probably connecting to and identifying with peoples that can only offer a very specific and limited view of the world. More recently the idea of Memes and Word Virus' have gained wider credence. This can lead to a broader view of what constitutes an ancestor. Memes can be taught to us from a variety of sources, and by this I do not mean to limit sources to humans of similar genetic background. Animals too may teach us behaviours, which we may learn to reinterpret in ways suitable to us. This art is part of the shamanic concept of animal ancestors, tribal totem animals and the practise of shape shifting. It also lies behind the use of animal forms in martial arts.

But we needn't stop at animals, plants can also teach us many things if we know how to listen, and again this is not a new concept. Peoples from around the world have cultivated traditions of forming spiritual relationships with plants and trees. Even viruses and bacteria may teach us things. Before what we narrowly define as life, before the first micro-organism began to multiply in the primal soup, existed great primal forces. Magicians

119

and mystics have referred to these as the elements. They survive in mythology as Giants, Titans, Dragons and Monsters. In the stories of Lovecraft they are represented as the Great Old Ones, the powerful and destructive forces that paradoxically created the universe and existed before the gods. Before the Great Old Ones exists only Chaos Unmanifest, an infinite void of non-existent possibility, the Ultimate Ancestor.

In this sense, the depiction of the creator as an 'All-Father' or 'All-Mother' doesn't seem so inaccurate, primitive or laughable. Although the assumption and projection of human consciousness and morality onto its nature is still a pathetically limited viewpoint.

Instead we should learn what we can from its nature. This is probably beyond the scope of Black Magic, and enters the realm of Chaos Magic in its purest state, that beyond and free of any particular paradigm or belief structure, including the one described in this book.

Related to necromancy is the magical concept of past and future lives. This subject has become so popular that it could be easy to dismiss it as a silly 'new age' fantasy. However, interesting results can be gained when working in a past life paradigm. One needn't believe in past lives in any kind of linear sense to make this work. My preference has been for the fractal model of 'shadow' selves throughout the space-time continuum, entities whose consciousness contain enough in common with your self that they could be considered to be 'previous' or 'future' versions of the self. In this sense it matters little if you look in the past, the future or sideways into a parallel universe to find your other self. Neither does it matter if the 'other' life you find really existed in our own 'objective' past, because they existed in a past somewhere in some reality. The easiest technique to use is visualisation. Have someone with you to ask questions and take notes. Describe what you see to them as you go through the visualisation. You could even use a tape-recorder for this. Use slow breathing to get into a trance. If you have others with you, mesmerism techniques can enhance this, they can run their hands about your body, never touching but remaining within a foot of contact. When you feel ready begin the visualisation by sitting up in your astral body and make your way outside. When able fly up into the sky and look around. Start to make time go backwards, slowly at first, by reversing the sun so it sets in the East where it rose. As you get used to this speed it up, until you find day and night are flashing by so fast you can no longer tell how many days are going by. Realise you are going to find a past self and slow the process down again until time is stopped. Drop down to wherever in the world the 'you that you are looking for' happens to be and enter their body. Let time move forward again. Say out loud what is happening, what you can see, feel, smell, hear. When you are ready leave by returning the way you came.

The vampire paradigm also fits nicely into the category of Black Magic. Psychic vampirism is a topic most magicians avoid, and even those that discuss it tend to start off with the assumption that it is an evil to be avoided. It is true that this kind of magic holds many dangers, and misused can lead to a morbid personality that is destructive of both itself and those around them. Yet there are dangers in all types of magic, and used correctly psychic vampirism can be a rewarding paradigm for the magician to make use of.

The topic of vampirism rightly deserves a whole book, and indeed there are some on the market. However, I will give a couple of examples of the uses author Jaq D Hawkins and myself have found for vampirism briefly here. It may surprise some that healing is a good use to put vampirism to. The method to use here is that of draining the victim of illness in order to feed the vampire. This method needs some caution, remember the intent is to drain the illness, not the patient. Also a certain amount of transformative magic is necessary when using this technique. Energy cannot be created or destroyed, but it can change states. The idea is to transmute the negative energy of the patient's illness into positive energy to 'feed' the vampire/magician.

Another use for vampirism is in servitor magic. One of the many problems faced by the servitor using magician is remembering to 'feed' the servitor. It is not always convenient and besides, the magician often has better things to do with their energy. A vampiric servitor on the other hand doesn't need feeding because it feeds itself, on the magicians enemies! An

121

enemy need not be defined as an individual. Draining the strength and power of oppressive establishments has proved popular. One needs to be careful with this kind of servitor however, because there have been cases where such a spirit ends up feeding and draining its creator. Such a situation is easy for an experienced magician to deal with, but can be problematic and self destructive to the beginner and the inexperienced, especially if they still retain much dualistic morality and preconceptions concerning the nature of vampires.

Death Magic Ritual

The following example of a Death magic ritual is based largely on Circuit VII of Leary's Eight Circuits, the concept being to launch oneself into space/zero gravity in order to gain access to the post terrestrial circuits of the mind. Consciousness is then raised through circuits five and six until circuit seven is reached. It is loosely structured, the idea being that each individual taking part will see their own representation of circuit seven.

Circuit Seven Death Spaceship Ritual

1. All taking part eat a small square of blotting paper, basically placebo acid. I'm not saying it can't be done with real acid, just that it isn't necessary to do so.

2. Count Down banishing. Everyone gets a clear space and crouches down, visualising themselves as rockets ready for blast off. Begin counting down from 10. "Ten – Nine – Eight – Seven – Six – Five – Four – Three – Two – One – We Have Ignition..." All visualise flames coming out of the bottom of the rockets and make rocket launch noises, suddenly accelerating into a jump as the critical pressure is reached.

3. Spinning in space. The space ships spin round and round really fast as they leave Earth's atmosphere. Spinning should be fast and continued for a good few minutes.

122

4. Fifth Circuit activates. Astronauts become aware of fifth circuit hedonic body consciousness by suddenly stopping spinning, sitting down in a foetal position and visualising themselves in Zero G space, floating about inside their space vessel. The ritual is best performed skyclad (naked), but it is not essential. Hands may be rubbed around ones own body to induce increased pleasure.

5. Sixth Circuit activates. Astronauts become aware of sixth circuit brain/neural consciousness. As dizziness fades, and self-pleasure becomes a sub-conscious reflex, the mind should become aware of its own internal archetypes. Ask each of these to show you the way to the Seventh circuit, the Ancestor/evolutionary/DNA circuit until one of them obliges.

6. Seventh Circuit activates. Here you can be in contact with your whole genetic past/present/future, your ancestors right back to the first single celled organisms, all future higher intelligence that will evolve from you. These ancestors and future descendants, may be able to offer you advice. Try and remember anything they tell you. Feel free to converse with them and ask questions.

7. Make notes. Some things you may want to make note of for your own personal, private reference, other things you may like to share with the group during de-briefing.

8. Re-entry. The space journey is over and the shuttle will re-enter the atmosphere. All assume re-entry positions and visualize the craft surrounded by flames as it re-enters. Then, each astronaut guides the craft back to the runway and lands it safely for re-use at a later date.

9. De-briefing. All astronauts may share any thoughts/messages they received with the rest of the group.

Purple Magic

With a simple wand and chalice you can perform the most chaotic conjuration of all - launch an entirely new person, and thus cheat death and throw bombs at the future. We sometimes wonder if the obsession of mediaeval and Renaissance sorcerers with creating golems and homunculi arose from their distaste at the sheer chaos and unpredictability of the simpler method of creating little monsters.

Peter J. Carroll[37]

Sex magic is about fertility and creativity. This energy can be channelled into the creation of children, animals, crops or works of art. This is not to say it is limited to these things, just that these are its more common uses. One thing to remember about fertility is that it is double sided. You want the crops to grow, but not the weeds. It is about giving birth to the wanted and preventing the growth of the unwanted. Acts of sensual Love can overlap into the realms of Sex and reproduction all too easily. Contraception is all important in keeping love-making and Sexual reproduction apart. Of course, in the human sense, gay sex is the ultimate contraceptive, but precautions still need to be taken to prevent other things from reproducing and spreading. Disease control is also important in the fertility of livestock and crops.

In art, disease is anything that compromises your creative flow, such as inhibitions, conformity, peer pressure, censorship. Censorship on the other hand can be used creatively, so long as each individual is free to censor their own input[38]. It is my life, therefore I should be able to choose what art I am subjected to. For example, I am mostly unimpressed with television, so I don't watch it. I don't like the way newspapers report the news, so I buy

---

37 Peter J Carroll, *'PsyberMagick: Advanced Ideas in Chaos Magick'* (Tempe, AZ, 1997) p. 76.
38 As Ramsey Dukes points out in 'What I Did In My Holidays'

'Private Eye' when I want to catch up on current affairs. I don't like the kind of radio friendly pop that they play on the radio, so I don't listen to it. Instead I put on CDs and records of my own choosing. If I only like certain songs by a band, I can make a tape of the album with the songs I don't like removed. Current technology allows us to compile MP3 collections of just the music we like. If I don't like conventional fashions in an area, say interior décor, I will find something more to my taste. It is me who has to live in my home after all, so it should look like what I want.

The fourth circuit in Leary's model, the social-moralistic circuit, corresponds to this area of magic. Within our own individuality we must decide on our choice of fashion, music, social group, sexual preferences, art. In other words, in order to have a fully developed fourth circuit, we must develop it fully within us as individuals, rather than let it be dictated to us by some establishment that thinks it knows better. Only when our inner, individual sense of social, sexual morality is strong are we truly free to explore the ecstasy and pleasure of the fifth circuit. Our creativity is in other words the foundation upon which our pleasure will be built.

Left to societies, or even to subcultures, art will inevitably lead to violence, conflict and ultimately war. It is through fashions in art, clothing and musical taste that cultures define themselves. It is through those definitions that cultures try and determine whether someone is 'one of us' or an 'outsider'. In a more sophisticated way war can also be fought in order to win the exotic art 'treasures' of the outsiders. Only through learning to identify with all subcultures and art styles can true peace be known. Not that a peaceful outlook is always to your personal advantage...

Red Magic

[Aggression] is a mode of problem-solving
that has been highly efficient for millions of years
of animal life. It is a curious thing that when we
dare to recognise that we have aggressive parts in
our mind's ecology, we will stand a good chance
of leading a happy and peaceful life. Aggression
can be useful. It can provide the power to
overcome obstacles, to break down restrictions...

Jan Fries[39]

War, like Death, is one of those areas of magic that has
acquired a very negative image. This kind of magic is actually
very much concerned with your physical securities and personal
and/or community boundaries. It is a magic of uniting processes,
specifically that form of union in which one set of processes
consumes another to feed itself. It is for this reason that many
gods of war grew out of what were previously fertility based
agricultural deities. This happened as civilisation dawned and
farming tribes sought to protect their investments in caring for
cattle and crops. The energy of Red magic is therefore mostly
concerned with two issues, that of protecting, defending your
personal space and that of ensuring you have enough food to
consume.

This kind of magic is one half of Circuit I in Leary's eight
circuits. It is food security and the fight or flight response. On the
one hand it concerns your predator within. The drive to acquire
those things you need for your survival. On the other it is your
fight or flight response to a potential threat. In other words it is
the half of circuit one concerned with your responses and drives to
insecurity. The other magic associated with Circuit I is Love
magic, and this concerns your reactions to feeling secure.

---

39 Jan Fries, 'Visual Magick', (Oxford, UK, 1992), pp. 153-
154.

In modern society it can be confusing for some as to how to stand up for yourself and protect your own interests. Instinct may tell you to run away or to kill the threat, but these options are often not very realistic, or even very desirable. Often in modern society such actions will find you a nice little secure personal space of your own in a prison cell. Security is an important drive in a modern human but it is not the only drive. Therefore we must learn to use more strategy in our approach to magical warfare. It has occurred to me that Sun Tzu's famous treatise on war 'The Art of War' can be adapted for use in Magical Combat. My magical interpretation of each chapter in this text follows.

01 Laying Plans

The meaning of the Chinese for this title refers to the deliberations in the temple selected by the general for his temporary use. In magical combat terms this is a stage of meditation, reflection and divination about the coming conflict. Sun Tzu lists five constant factors to bear in mind.

i. Moral Law. This refers to harmony or balance. One must make sure, when enlisting allies, be they fellow magicians, God-forms and/or servitors, that they are in harmony with your motivations and ideology so that no inner conflicts may arise.

ii. Heaven. What outside influences are likely to have an effect on the outcome of battles, and the overall war? What astrological influences are there? What do other divinatory methods tell you? Which influences can be used to your advantage, and what warnings can be read?

iii. Earth. This concerns distances and terrain. In magical combat, this is to be read symbolically. Are you fighting on a psychological, political, ideological, financial, legal or some other ground? Are several types of terrain available? Where are ambushes likely? Where can you lay ambush? Where are good places for open battles?

iv. Commander. The five virtues of a good commander

are Wisdom, Sincerity, Benevolence, Courage and Self Respect/Control. Before the combat begins is a good time to reflect on your own strengths and weaknesses in these areas, but a truly wise general would also reflect on the strengths and weaknesses of their opponent.

v.   Method and Discipline. This reflects how well you are able to organise and discipline the forces at your disposal. The magical discipline of dealing with war gods or attack and defensive servitors cannot be exactly likened to organising an army but nonetheless discipline and method are important. Now is a good time to reflect on your magical discipline, methods and control. Is your opponent also magical? If not then what methods and disciplines will they be using to counter you?

02 Waging War

This chapter is about preparations and the planned length of a campaign. Do not rush into battle. Make sure enough time has been spent in preparations, in laying plans and gathering required resources. At the same time make sure the war is not drawn out into a lengthy campaign. In magical combat, as in actual war, a lengthy campaign will only drain your resources, strength and time, leaving you open to attack from other quarters, or even from within.

Let your attack servitors feed off your enemy's resources and keep your enemy's treasure as rewards. Make your object victory, not lengthy campaigns.

03 Attack by Stratagem

It is better to capture your enemies forces than to destroy them. Pre-empt and counter your enemies strategy. It should be easy to do this against a non-magical opponent. For a magical enemy divination and scrying may need to be employed. Guard against such techniques from a magical opponent. Avoid attacking 'walled cities'. Use magical seduction techniques to cause your opponent to be lead astray into more vulnerable positions.

Try to subdue the enemy without any fighting. If you are really successful you can win the war and end up with your opponent as a friend, although this is an unlikely outcome of magic to magic combat. To do this you need to defeat the 'government' whilst doing no harm to the 'people'. In a magical sense this can refer to winning by destroying the 'aggressor' persona of your opponent, whilst leaving the rest of the individual/organisation unharmed. Thus subdued you may end up with a new friend, albeit initially a rather servile one.

04 Tactical Dispositions

Conceal the condition of your 'forces'. In a magical combat sense this refers to making sure the weaknesses and strengths of your servitors are undiscovered. This is only really an issue against a magically aware opponent, although there are often individuals with no magical interest who are a little naturally psychic. Beware of the forces you could accidentally unleash in such people because it can be extremely dangerous.

Fall on the enemy when they are least prepared to fight and give them no time in which to respond. Modify tactics to meet those of your opponent.

05 Energy

In this chapter, Sun Tzu discussed the importance of hidden and revealed intentions. Sometimes hidden attacks can pose as revealed attacks and vice versa. The importance of this is to never let your opponent work out what you are doing. If you want to do the obvious, make your opponent suspect the deceptive. If you plan a sneak attack, make it look like you are doing something understandable.

Speed and judgement are also of key importance here. When a new opening appears, be ready to quickly exploit it. But have judgement to do so only at exactly the right moment, and be sure that the opening isn't a trap laid by your adversary.

There is also a method of hate gnosis here. Build up anger but refuse to release it. Just let it build up and build up. Feed it with all the hate and anger you can muster. Let your impatience be held in check, like the force in a crossbow. Then exert control in the crucial moment of the ritual to release the anger in one concentrated burst. It must be exactly the correct moment to strike, or all the effort is wasted. However, since in magic 'the correct moment' is a subjective thing, this shouldn't pose too much of a problem. One idea might be to pre-arrange a signal, perhaps a steady drum roll could be going during the build up, with the release signal being the sudden stopping of the drums...

06 Weak Points and Strong

An enemy that has time to think is in a good defensive position. When you strike you must strike with surprise, in points that are undefended, weakly defended or can only be defended in haste. Trick your opponent into rash decisions. Avoid the well defended, since you will waste your energy and your forces.

Make sure your own defence covers attacks from unexpected angles. Be strong in all areas of your life. Make sure all weak points are well defended. Overall be like water and take the path of least resistance. Flow away from high insurmountable places and attack downhill. Don't waste energy trying to defend the undefendable and don't bother to attack the well defended.

07 Manoeuvring

Making sure you are harmonised within before engaging with your enemy. If your own self is in two minds about how to proceed then your chances of success are significantly reduced. Neither-neither and gnosis techniques can be used to bring about a focus and remove doubts. Fire and forget formula are also useful. Again, look at the morals of the magical systems from which your servitors originate. Are your aims in harmony with the aims and moral outlook of your spirits?

When you are harmonised within, your manoeuvring should be much simpler.

08 Variation in Tactics

Vary the tactics you use to avoid becoming predictable. Avoid moving through vulnerable positions where you may be taken by surprise. Avoid falling foul of the five faults of a general...

i) Recklessness - don't let your opponent entice you into rash decisions which may prove fatal.

ii) Cowardice - don't hold back your strength when it is necessary to strike.

iii) Hasty Temper - don't be provoked by insults.

iv) Delicacy of Honour, sensitive to shame - don't let your sense of honour be exploited.

v) Over solicitude for servitors - sometimes some servitors will need to engage in battle which will threaten their existence. However, if you hold back out of fear for their safety, you may put them in greater danger. It is rare magical battle gets this complex, but it is as well to be aware of the possibilities. By extension this may also apply to losses in other areas of your life. Don't be to attached to things you might lose in the course of war or you can lose focus and hope.

These weaknesses should also be observed in your opponent. Which of these five faults can you observe in your foe? In what ways can you exploit those weaknesses?

09, 10 & 11 The Army on the March, Terrain and The Nine Situations

These chapters are mostly concerned with the terrain, places to camp, the physical types of terrain, the tactical types of terrain, areas to avoid, and the types of tactics to use in each. These do not translate exactly to magical combat. It is nonetheless a good idea to learn the concepts and apply the type of thinking involved to your own fight. What map are you fighting on? Psychological, Political, Ideological, Legal, Financial?

Make sure you don't lose communication with your servitors. Keep them well supplied, let them drain their energy requirements from your foe. Cut off your opponents important communication and supply routes. Avoid getting into hopelessly entangled situations where it looks like you can't make a right move. If you need to stall for time, get the battle onto ground where neither side wants to attack. Create a temporary stale mate situation.

Where can you prepare ambushes for your foe? What places may your foe have set traps for you?

12 The Attack by Fire

i)   Burn enemy encampments
ii)   Burn their stores
iii)   Burn their means of supply
iv)   Burn their weapons
v)   Rain a volley of fire upon them

When using fire in a ritual, especially a war rite, make sure you have used required safety precautions. Make flammable effigies of your foe, their servitors, their homes, their stores, their supplies and their weapons. Summon fire elementals to your aid and burn them. Send the fire elementals out to make swift and devastating sneak attacks.

13 The Use of Spies

One may be aware at this point that the chapters in 'The Art of War' are not to be followed as some kind linear formula. Understand all the principles of each and apply them simultaneously. This final chapter is therefore not something you use to conclude the war, unless perhaps you are losing and need to use trickery and diplomacy to win a favourable peace treaty, cease-fire or truce.

While engaged in battle of any kind you must know your enemy. Many of the previous chapters made mention of information gathered about various aspects of your foe. This information comes from spies. In magical combat one of your most unique and powerful spies is your own preferred divination method. At the same time hard facts from an inside source can be of invaluable help.

Green Magic

Love has no other desire than to fulfil itself.
But if you love and must needs have desires,
let these be your desires:
To melt and be like a running brook
that sings its melody to the night.
To know the pain of too much tenderness.
To be wounded by your own understanding of love;
And to bleed willingly and joyfully.
Kahlil Gibran[40]

Love magic is magic concerned with co-operative union, where two doings come together to create a third greater doing. In practise this need not be limited to just two coming together, as any magician familiar with egregor magic will know. The main areas of interest in Green, or love magic can be discussed in four main areas, Erotic love, friendship, Self-Love and egregor formation. An egregor being an entity that results from the interaction of and relationship between two or more other entities.

Most magicians would consider that Erotic love falls more into the category of Purple, or sex magic. Or that it is at least a combination of the two. Personally, given the creative 'fertility' associations of purple magic, I would suggest leaving purple out of the equation unless you are planning on children, or are in the kind of relationship where it doesn't matter (such as a same sex relationship). Even then if you do use purple magic in this way, be careful to direct the creative magic away from anything unwanted. It can be used to good effect in the creation of servitors of various kinds, and the egregor of a loving partnership is renewed and strengthened using such a method.

So what is the egregor of a loving union? If you were to take the two individuals and observed their behaviours you would notice that they undergo many changes in personality and behaviour under different conditions, even if they consider

---

40 Kahlil Gibran, *'The Prophet'* (St Ives, UK, 1992), pp. 16-17.

themselves to still be 'I' throughout. One such set of conditions is where the situation concerns the couple. Each of the two individuals will, when making decisions that have consequences for the relationship, consider what their partner might want. If the egregor is strong then the couple will be easily able to anticipate each others needs and desires, and the needs and desires of the egregor, and will be able to make decisions which are mutually beneficial.

If the egregor is weak, it may try to compensate by bullying the two individuals into compliance in order to ensure its own survival. If this works then although the couple may stay together for a long time, it is unlikely that either individual would be happy. In such a situation, both individuals in the couple spend so much of their time and effort in trying to make their 'relationship' better, usually by trying to please their partner, and expecting the reverse, that they forget that happiness can only be created within. Outside stimuli can only entice you to create your own happiness, if you are willing.

Jan Fries describes what can happen when two members of a couple expect each other to provide their happiness, which he claims actually comes from chemicals we induce ourselves in our brains...

'We fell in love' sounds much more romantic than saying 'you made yourself love me while I made myself love you', let alone suggesting that the loving feelings do not come from the partner but are induced by one's own brain. In our upside-down world, people like to believe that love comes and goes as fate has it, and usually enough, at some point, both partners get bored, stop loving one another, and blame her/him for 'having changed' or some such crime. That lovers' quarrels can be so vicious may well be due to the fact that here we have two addicts who blame each other for having stopped the supply of happiness-inducing chemicals.

I believe the theory that we can love who we want is part of the whole picture but not the whole. If we consciously decide that we will love someone, then we can no doubt create that illusion in

135

our heads quite successfully that we do. We can program our minds to respond positively to that person's presence, creating all the right 'feel-good' chemicals and hormones, and feeling very much 'in Love'. The questions can be 'is it worth it', 'is it ethical' and such like.

Such exercises can be very rewarding, since if one has never truly experienced love, or for that matter a bad relationship, then there is no better teacher of these things than experience. If you are capable of making yourself love someone that you don't love deep down, how much better at it will you be when you find someone your deep mind wants you to love? Failed attempts at loving relationships are not really failures but important and transformative experiences. The more you practice being 'in love' the better you'll be when the time comes. And if the time never comes? At least you will have lived the illusion that it had and experienced something...

What about the ethics of pretending to love someone you don't? It is not for me to preach what ethics you should and shouldn't have. To my mind these are personal decisions we all have to make for ourselves. My own view has been that it largely depends upon the exact nature of the situation. I would not now marry or move in with someone whom I did not love deep down, because if my subconscious has decided not to love them, it has probably worked something out I haven't. Going against the warning of the subconscious in this instance may well end in disaster.

Which brings me to what happens when you don't consciously force yourself to love someone. In this case the decision is left to your subconscious, which is much more efficient in working out whether you will be happy. For this reason you will find many people that you meet whom your subconscious doesn't tell you to love, and you will also sense subconscious reservations about many people you want to love.

But is your subconscious always right? How does it know what makes you happy? Can you change what makes you happy? I think your subconscious is pretty accurate, given that you have supplied it with accurate data. You may have never deeply considered what you want in the opposite sex and only have a sort of static image of doll-like desirable beauty and soft/firm flesh. In this case it is unlikely your subconscious will anticipate that a real life partner is a human being, with their own unique personality. Worse, it may try to set you up in a life long relationship with an inflatable and/or vibrating friend. All magicians need to explore their own minds and work out what hidden needs and desires they should resolve to find in life, including their loving mate (or mates, who am I to say you only need one?).

Mix Green with Blue to put the pleasure into love. What games do you and your partner like playing? Do you play them enough? What games would you both secretly like to play? What toys would help enhance these games? Many people try out a variety of games, including, but not limited to, bondage, role-play, dominance-submission, spanking, whipping, food-play, dressing up, strip-dancing, 'swinging' parties, SM play parties, animal pretend play, posing for photos/camcorders, strip games (such as poker). If you can't have fun with the one you love, who can you have fun with? The games don't have to be limited to sexual games however, if you and your partner like to go out and play darts, badminton, tennis, pool, dungeons and dragons or cards, then do so. Fun is where you make it. It doesn't even have to be a game, going out can be fun. Pubs, clubs, theatres, cinemas and restaurants can all be fun.

We choose friends in a very similar manner, although we tend to be less cautious here because under normal conditions we don't have to live with our friends, or have so much invested in them. On rare occasions your subconscious will warn you about certain potential friends, or even current ones. You would do well to listen to your subconscious at this point because you may find the 'friend' is no friend at all, or at the very least something is brewing that could see you falling out if you don't discuss your feelings of misgiving. Even then you may still fall out. At other times your deep mind may warn you that someone is neurotic and needy to a parasitic degree or that they are smothering and trying to make you dependent upon them. Other than this it is often very useful and very informative to have friends who are quite different from yourself and with widely different points of view.

In attracting both Erotic love and Platonic friendships, the concept of beauty can be an important one. The first thing to remember is that 'Beauty is in the eye of the beholder'. But what does this mean? What exactly is beauty and where does it arise? What do we mean when we say something is beautiful? When we talk of beauty we mostly mean a visual aesthetic. In itself, people and objects do not have a visual aesthetic until there is an observer. Light rebounds off the subject, but this in itself is not beautiful except perhaps to a physicist/mathematician who can visualise the complex equations involved. Some of the light then passes in the direction of the observer and enters the eyes. But even in the eyes there is no concept of beauty, except to the biologist who can appreciate the wonders of the processes involved. The eye is simply a light and colour sensitive organ. Various receptors in the eyes are stimulated by the light and simply pass the information to the brain. It is in the brain of the observer that the subjective quality of relative beauty or lack thereof is assessed.

I realised this at quite an early age and so began my first magical experiment, although I was too young to appreciate that that is what I was doing at the time. My logic was that if beauty was in my own mind, I could decide for myself what was beautiful and what was ugly. Since I decided that it was not a pleasant thing to live in an ugly world, I decided to try and see beauty in everything and everyone! Amazingly it worked, although it took me a long time to appreciate the beauty in a lot of truly horrifying things. Being able to watch horror films without anything bad happening helps the imprint and helps build a positive, excited imprint in response to terror.

Imprinting plays a large part in what we consider 'beauty' to be. Large portions of society may end up imprinting contemporary fashions as their concept of beauty, others may react negatively to the 'norm' and attach to this or that 'subculture'. This is mostly superficial and random. Most individuals have let random circumstance tell them how to perceive things, rather than working out what is best for themselves. A 'Chaos of the Normal'. A magician must be able to transcend this and free themselves from its restrictive bonds. The magician can walk between various aesthetics as it pleases

138

them to do so, walking between the worlds (of fashions and subcultures) and being able to feel comfortable in a wide range of different peoples, and perhaps more importantly having them feel comfortable with the magician's presence.

So how does a magician approach changing their attitudes to aesthetics? One way would be to begin with the self. How much beauty do you see in yourself? Practise seeing your own beauty in front of a mirror. The more beauty you see, the more your facial muscles will respond to the positive and negative signals you give yourself, avoiding 'ugly' combinations and getting better at producing 'beautiful' ones. Then try other people. This is perhaps easiest with complete strangers on the street or someone you trust a lot. Look at them as if they are really attractive. Make yourself believe they are. Don't slobber or approach this with sleaze in mind, just appreciate the visual aesthetic. You will perhaps find that some people will look back at you. Don't be shy, this is actually helpful. Some people will look away embarrassed, perhaps with a smile on their face, or a blush. This is good, many people look more attractive in this state, so not only are you learning to see beauty where you couldn't before, you are also making things actually transform and become more beautiful and pleasing. Looking at people as if they are attractive will make them more so as it will increase, perhaps just little, their own self-image. More importantly though, it will give you courage and confidence in your own ability to be attractive to other people. Don't be deceived by media images of fashionable youthful beauty. If you fit that stereotype, you can enhance it by using these techniques to make your inner beauty shine through.

If on the other hand you don't fit the stereotype, then revealing your inner beauty may be the only way to overcome peoples media induced prejudices. Never tell them they are being politically incorrect, this will make you appear aggressive and ugly and exactly the opposite of what you are trying to appear. Seduction doesn't work that way.

There is more to self-love, and indeed the love of others, than simply the perception of visual, audio, and olfactory beauty, although all the senses have a strong part to play. When you begin to get more intimate with someone, or indeed yourself, taste

139

and touch can also come into play. Look after your skin. Eat foods that have enjoyably sensuous flavours for you. If traditional aphrodisiacs such as oysters make you feel sick, then don't eat them, because feelings of nausea are not very sexy. Perhaps you would find a creamy chocolate mouse more helpful, or a dish of freshly cooked garlic, red onions, tomatoes, pasta shells, olive oil, minced beef (or lentils) and Italian herbs. Then again it can all depend on whether you enjoy the taste of garlic through the skin...

Even with all the right sensory signals in place there could be something missing. Self-love requires more than just finding yourself beautiful. You must feel happy and secure in yourself. Without this any security you get from elsewhere can always be lost. Security with yourself from within will be with you wherever you go. This same security can also be important with your lovers and your friends, but it never comes without a price. Once you have won self-love it becomes easier to win the true love of others. But if the other does not possess self-love in themselves then they may still fail to truly love you in return. True love is not neurotic of potential future loss, but lives in the present and creates a bond of security in the moment. Neurotic fear of loss is a symptom of sentimentality, not true love.

Love Magic Ritual

This is a simple rite which can be elaborated on and adjusted for work on Self-Love, the love of your lover and even just love on a friendship level. If you are practising Self-Love, then begin this work in front of a mirror. If you are with a lover, then sit on your bed opposite each other, naked perhaps. If you are with a friend or friends, sit opposite each other in an arrangement where everyone can see everyone else.

Throughout this ritual you must cease to talk in words. You must use your voice to intone feeling and emotion only. Use your eyes and facial expressions to convey your feelings of love, friendship, companionship and trust with either yourself, your lover or your friends.

Follow the following simple steps...

Ritual

❶   The ritual space is prepared using a suitable banishing rite.

❷   All present close their eyes and intone a random pre-chosen sound and repeat until that sound becomes forgotten and the voice is naturally intoning a whole variety of meaningless sounds.

❸   Close eyes and use these random sounds to communicate to your inner self. Express how much you love that self and ask it to guide your communication and expression of emotion throughout the rest of the ritual.

❹   Open eyes and look at your target. Express the sounds, gestures and facial expressions that just come naturally. Avoid recognisable words if possible, or at the very least avoid recognisable sentences.

❺   Go wherever the rite leads. If you are on your own it may lead to masturbation, if you are with your lover it might lead to a passionate cuddle and/or sex. If you are with friends it may culminate in a group hug. But these are only some of the possibilities, you will probably know when the rite is over however...

Fractal Chaos — The Chaos of the Normal

Work

Death

The Baby Dragon is Hatched

Earth

Air

Sex

Play

Ego

Be

Do

War

Fire

Water

Psyche

Love

Æther — The Egg Hatches

Primal Ings — The roots of All

6. The Kaos Hieroglyph

Imagine the horizon line stretching out into a tree. Make of that
tree, grown in a purely human space, our shared orientation, our
next place to go, our common purpose. Then Gaia the egg may
crack and the winged serpent/tree will emerge: a new dimension.
Aloas Kino 01[41]

The Eight Rayed Star of Chaos

The Chaosphere, or eight-rayed star of Chaos is one of the
most secret of all occult symbols. The majority of people are
familiar with the pentagram and its occult significance these days,
even if they are not particularly interested in the occult. Many
magicians and pagans however can be unaware of the Chaosphere
unless they have had some contact with Chaos Magic. This
despite the fact that many children and teenagers will know of the
symbol from their role-playing games, comics, fantasy novels and
the various music CDs that have used it.

Over the years I have decided to make a study of the
history behind the chaosphere and what it has represented over
time. I began by looking for evidence of the eight-rayed star that
many modern goddess worshippers claim is the Star of Ishtar or
Star of Inanna. In all my researches I have still found no hard
evidence that this is the case, the earliest reference I have seen
dating only last century and coming from the literature of the
'Fellowship of Isis'[42]. This attribution appears to have been gained
by 'divine inspiration' or an act of illumination on the part of
Olivia Robertson. The FOI literature is a little unclear on this
point, so its association with Ishtar may indeed be older. In any
case, an eight rayed star has been associated with Mary, in her
guise as 'Star of the Sea'. It may be that she inherited the star

---

41 Aloas Kino 01, *'Breathing on the Goat's Perineum: Thee
Spelling ov Magic(k)'*, (Internet)

42 see *'The College of Isis Manual'* by Olivia Robertson.

from Ishtar. This may especially be the case if the theory that the three Mary's of the gospel stories are all Ishtar's priestesses has some truth to it.

According to my researches, the star was used in Babylon, but does not appear to have been especially specific to Ishtar. Many of the Babylonian gods have been depicted with the symbol. Eventually I came upon a source suggesting an even older origin. Whilst reading a book on the origins of civilisation I came across an ancient Mesopotamian pictogram of an eight-rayed star. This dates as far back as 3100 BCE and is believed to be an early symbol representing the words/concept of 'star', 'divinity' and 'sky'. Here we can observe the early connection of stars with deities, and the sky or heavens with the home of the gods.

By around 2500 BCE the symbol became used in cuneiform writing, being only slightly stylised. By the time of Ancient Babylon around 1800 BCE, the diagonal rays became shorter, or stunted, with the cross shape predominating. By the time of Assyria in 700 BCE the diagonals have disappeared completely leaving just an upright cross as the symbol representing divinity. By the time Christians began using the symbol it was nearly a thousand years old in that form. The fact that Christian mythology has Jesus born under an eight-rayed star, and ending his life on a cross may be a metaphor for the transformation of this important symbol.

| Early Pictograph | Cuneiform | Babylon | Assyria |
| 3100 BCE | 2500 BCE | 1800 BCE | 700 BCE |

Meanwhile, eight rayed designs have appeared in Europe. Jan Fries gives some examples in his book 'Helrunar – A manual of rune magick'. The earliest eight spoked design dates from the Neolithic Alps, sometime from c.5000BC. It is not clear what it may have meant, or even if there existed a standard meaning in those days. It may have meant different things to different people at different times. The shape doesn't resemble a star, instead resembling eight 'Mannaz' runes radiating from a central circle.

Fries gives examples of more star like Neolithic designs from Scandinavia from c.2500BC. One of these designs incorporates a 'dot' or circle at the centre, from which the eight rays radiate. Again it is not clear what meaning these forms had in Neolithic times, but it is possible that they were connected with ideas about stars and the night sky.

Neolithic Alps
c5000 BCE

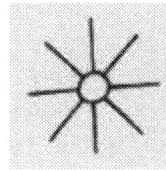

Neolithic Scandinavia
c2500 BCE

On the other side of the Atlantic, the Aztecs used eight rayed discs to represent the sun. The Aztecs whose origins are in the early 12th century, typically used a circle, with eight triangles emanating from it, as a symbol of the sun. Sometimes this was a relatively simple device, although still more complex than the Mesopotamian or Neolithic symbols, while at other times it was carved in intricately detailed and complex patterns that rival or even far surpass the detail of the gothic cathedral sculpture used in Europe during the same period.

The eight trigrams of the I-Ching are a more complex system of symbols that are often arranged in a circular fashion in the eight directions. Its origins lay in China c3000BCE. If one were to equate 'yin' with '-', negative and 'being' and 'yang' with '+', positive and 'doing' then a correspondence could be made between the trigrams and the eight directions of the Kaosphere. Such a correspondence would not directly relate to traditional I-Ching but some illumination may be gained from considering the relationship between Ch'ien and Love, Sun and War, Tui and Work, K'an and Play, Li and Sex, Kên and Death, Chên and Ego, K'un and Psyche. Or if you prefer, you can use Crowley's Qabalistic correspondences to the I-Ching (replacing Earth with Neptune) to work out that Chien is Death, K'an is Sex, Sun is Work, Tui is Play, Kên is Love, Chên is War, Li is Ego and K'un is Psyche.

Neither the Fu Hsi Arrangement, nor the King Wen

147

Arrangements seem to relate to the Kaosphere, so I humbly offer the Crowley and Chan Ning Arrangements for anyone who may be interested...

Crowley Arrangement

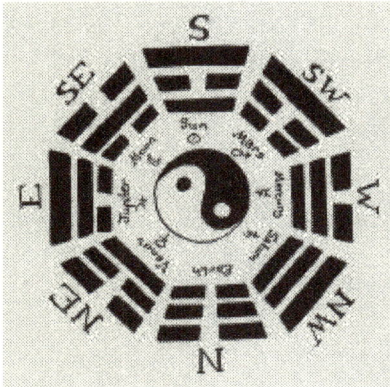

Chan Ning Arrangement

1944 CE
(Arranged for Kaosphere
2001 CE)

2001 CE

Coming forward into more recent magical history, we may choose to look at eight pointed devices used by Crowley and Spare. In Crowley's 'Thoth Tarot' we may notice first that the star on the coin of the Magus, the star of Mercury, is eight sided. In fact it is a unicursal octagram. This symbol reappears in the Ten of Disks as the coin in Netzach. The Eight of Wands also bears a design worthy of attention in a study of the chaosphere's origins. This design shows eight jagged rays of lightning emanating from a central point, and tipped with arrows like the chaosphere.

The card is also connected to Mercury. Crowley connects it with ideas about electricity, light, speech and rainbows. He intends it to represent the energy of high velocity.

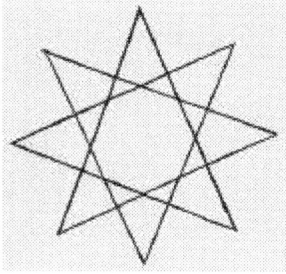

Unicursal Octagram
(Star of Mercury)
1944 CE

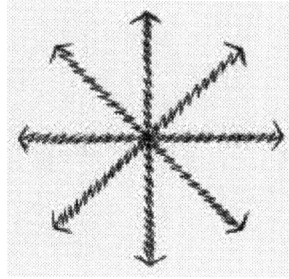

Eight of Wands

1944 CE

In Earth Inferno by Austin Osman Spare can be found a design with remarkable similarity to the modern Chaosphere shape. KIA sits at the centre inside a circle, in the form of a vulture's head. Eight rays emanate from KIA and reach an outer circle. Four of these rays are tipped with arrows. The upwards pointing arrow also has branches into three near the top, causing it to resemble a Mannaz rune. Each of the eight directions is labled, starting from the top these are...

Top most: A & Ω.
Top (right branch): Death (into) illusion.
Top Right: Rehersal.
Right: Rehersal.
Bottom Right: Lifes Nightmare.
Bottom: Destiny Birth and Fortune.
Bottom Left: Dwellers on the threshold.
Left: The Chaos of the Normal.
Top Left: Despair.
Top (left branch): Birth (out-of) illusion.

A simple reproduction is printed below, but the reader is advised to consult the original for complete detail.

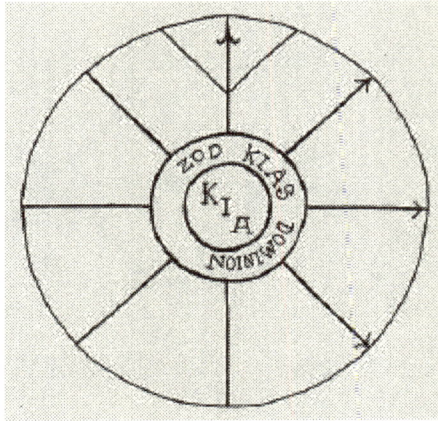

Synopsis of Inferno (Austin Osman Spare)
1905 CE

Neopagans, Druids and Wiccans use a system known as the 'Wheel of the Year'. This divides the year into eight and maps it to the eight main compass points. The Winter Solstice is considered to be North, where it is cold, and the Summer Solstice the south where it is warm. Obviously a different set of directions are used in the Southern Hemisphere. The festivals are based on the agricultural year, and have little connection to modern life, and so the system has little way of gaining any kind of power. Many pagans realise this and try to 'reconnect with nature', as if an agricultural life is in any way more natural than an office job. For the purposes of creating eight festivals of Chaos, I have gone more by feeling and come up with the following correspondences, starting from Samhain/Halloween. Exact dates are not given, plenty of books provide contradictory advice on this. I leave it up to the individual to use this information as it suits them.

Samhain is a festival of Death, a celebration of the dead, of our ancestors. It is also a good time to connect with future descendants, perhaps higher intelligence, highly evolved beings that will contact us as their ancestors. This is a time of fun, of dressing up in images of horror, death and the macabre. It is a time for tricks and a time for treats. Demonic faces and sigils can be carved into pumpkins. It is a good time for death curses and healing. Remember, not all of our ancestors are human, we eventually all derive from single celled organism that formed out of DNA, if the current scientific paradigm is to be believed. DNA itself formed out of primal molecular, atomic and quantum forces which themselves were spawned by the Primal Chaos itself. Chaos is our ultimate ancestor.

The Winter Solstice is a festival of the Psyche. It is the time of year of longest night and shortest day, the majority of people take time off work and are more able to give their inner selves a chance to express themselves. Maybe that's why so many families find this time of Year so stressful. A magician, who should have a good relationship with their subconscious selves, should find the time more relaxing. Traditionally, presents are exchanged, cards are given out, and lots of rich food, cakes, puddings, pies and sweets are eaten. Lots of alcohol is usually consumed, including stronger forms of alcohol rarely drunk by most people the rest of the year round.

Imbolc is a festival of Love. It is traditional to send 'Valentine' cards around this time of year, propose marriages and reaffirm existing Love with cards, flowers and presents. It may also be a good time to think of the other kinds of love that are important to us in our lives. Close family members, good friends and basically anyone important to us in our lives.

The Spring Equinox is a festival of Play. The year is beginning to warm up. Easter holidays are around this time. Children are able to play outside more. Images of Eggs and Bunny's abound all over, and many chocolate eggs may be found. (As an aside, Cadbury's Cream Eggs have an eight pointed star on each side. Although by far my favourite chocolate egg is Green and Black's Maya Gold, which is organic and fair trade in addition to being delicious.) After this point the days are longer than the nights. Darkness continues to wane and Light continues to wax.

151

Beltaine is a festival of Sex. Traditional rites of this time involve wild love making in the woods, dancing about phallic May-poles and vaginal Hawthorne trees. This is a time of fertility and creativity and is a good time for artistic pursuits and wild sex.

The Summer Solstice is a festival of Ego. The Sun is at the peak of its power, daylight hours at their yearly peak. People begin to spend warm holidays on beaches, clad in minimal attire, outwardly expressing themselves the most they will all year. Chilled beer, ice-cream and days at the sea side are all traditional rituals of this time of year, as are staying in tents and caravans, open air rock festivals, travelling abroad, and eating barbecues. It is a good time of year for strawberries, peaches and nectarines.

Lammas is a War festival. This festival still has a link to the agricultural cycle. At Lammas the corn king is slain so his blood will ensure the fertility of the crops. This ritual is about ensuring we have enough food to eat. It is about protecting our food resources from invaders, be they foreign humans, animal pests or even weeds, bacteria and infections. We may also choose to try to protect our food from what we see as harmful agricultural practises, such as poisonous pesticides and artificial fertilisers. On another level it is a time for political protest (although this goes on all year).

The Autumn Equinox is a Work festival. This can be seen in relation to the school/college and university year, when it is about the time a new academic year starts, although in a general sense it is a time when the main holiday season comes to a close. In an agricultural sense this is a festival of the harvest, and obviously a lot of work has to be done to get the crops picked, preferably before they get over-ripe. After this point Darkness Continues to wax in power and light continues its wane. Which leads us back to Samhain, traditionally seen as the end/beginning of the Pagan year.

The Sigil of Chaos, in the eternal champion books of Michael Moorcock, is probably the first description of the Chaosphere as we now know it, although Michael may have been influenced by any number of the above symbols mentioned, or even some I have neglected to include.

The Warhammer games of Games Workshop seem to

152

have borrowed the symbol from Moorcock's writings. It is probable that Carroll took the symbol from Moorcock also, although I have also heard rumours that he collected gaming figurines (and may still do if the rumours are correct!). To my knowledge, Carroll was the first to publicly name the symbol the 'Chaosphere' and the first to suggest a three dimensional variant of the symbol (a sphere with eight arrows pointing to the corners of a cube). All in all, the symbol appears to have a very rich historical background encompassing a wide range of ideas and philosophies. Which is somewhat fitting.

The Monas Hieroglyph

The Monas Hieroglyph was a symbol created by the famous Elizabethan alchemist, Dr John Dee. Dee is more famous for his discovery/creation of the Enochian language, the language of the angels (with the help of his assistant Kelly). The hieroglyph however is a much more theoretical piece of alchemy, and is taken from Dee's Monas Hieroglyphica (The Hieroglyphic Monad). It is essentially a symbol showing a stylised version of Alchemical Mercury at the centre of an egg. An egg symbolised two things to Alchemists, and these were the Philosophers Egg, another name for Mercury, and the Cosmic Egg, another name for the Solar System.

The Philosophers egg was the result of the union of the Solar Cock (Sulphur) and Lunar Hen (Salt). It was made up of the four elements, the shell being Earth, the clear membrane between shell and white being Air, the white being Water and the yolk being Fire. The Cosmic Egg represented the union of the seven known planetary energies. Thus the egg represented macrocosmic Mercury/Ether/Quintessence as the central figure represented the magician, microcosmic Mercury/Gnosis/Illumination.

I have explained in chapter three how the alchemical symbol for Mercury appears to be made up of all four elements, and all ten planetary energies. Basically, if we examine the glyphs used by the alchemists to represent the planets, we find that they are composed of four basic shapes that represent the four elements. None of the ten planets contain all four components, and thus do not represent the completion or balance of the elements. Neither Salt nor Sulphur are properly balanced either, Salt containing only Circle and Crescent, Sulphur containing only Cross and Arrow. Mercury (not planetary Mercury) however shows all four in combination. The common symbol for Aether, a six spoke wheel, represents the harmony of the seven classical planets. The Sun is at the centre and the other six planets orbit around it. Thus Mercury is equivalent to Ether or Quintessence, and is transcendent of the duality of Sulphur and Salt, the four Elements and the ten planetary energies. Uranus is the planet whose energies most closely resemble Aether/Mercury, however on its own its energies can be considered an astral reflection, an imperfect copy of the thing it represents, a flawed version of the original aetheric pattern.

The Monas Hieroglyph then is a symbol of the monotheist aeon magician, monolithic, whole, complete and in perfect and mystical union with a whole complete and balanced universe.

The Kaos Hieroglyph

The Kaos Hieroglyph is a new symbol I have created that combines the ideas of the Kaosphere with the Monas Hieroglyph. The egg of the monolithic universe is hatching, the magician's many selves are pouring out in all directions. The universe becomes a multiverse. The prison of static balance gives way to the freedom of a strange attractor equilibrium. Use this symbol as you will...

Appendix A

Aeonics

There are far too many systems of aeonics already out there for me to want to add to the confusion. Perhaps instead if I offer a rough chart, showing how the existing systems may fit together. I have also included how they might correspond to the Kaosphere. The German names for the Discordian Aeons are also included, and are taken from the Illuminatus trilogy, where a fictional Adam Weishaupt (founder of the Bavarian Illuminati) is credited with their invention.

Kaosphere	Discordianism	Crowley / Maatian	Carroll	Leary Circuit
Level of 0 Chaos Unmanifest	Verwirrung Chaos	Nameless	Shamanic	I
Level of 1 Ether	Zweitracht Discord	Isis	Pagan	II
Level of 2 Duality	Unordnung Confusion	Osiris	Monotheist	III
Level of 4 Elemental Materialism	Beamtenherrschaft Bureaucracy	Horus	Rationalist	IV
Level of 8 Super-Sensual Hedonism	Grummet Aftermath	Maat	Pandemonic	V
Level of Bifurcation Fractal Chaos		Wordless		VI
				VII
				VIII

157

Appendix B

Eight Circuit Model

Throughout this book I have made comparisons between the Kaosphere and Leary's Eight Circuits. The following table is an easy reference of my correspondences, for your convenience.

Cybermorphic Kaosphere	Eight Circuit Model
Green Magic – Love	Circuit I – Security/
Red Magic – War	Survival Mind
Yellow Magic – Ego	Circuit II – Dominant Mind
Orange Magic – Work	Circuit III – Semantic Mind
Purple Magic – Sex	Circuit IV – Hive Mind
Blue Magic – Play	Circuit V – Body Mind
White Magic – Psyche	Circuit VI – Neural Mind
Black Magic – Death	Circuit VII – DNA Mind
Octarine Magic – Aetherics	Circuit VIII – Quantum Mind

Appendix C

Cybermorphic Kaosphere Training

This system works through all the aspects of the cybermorphic kaosphere in order to familiarise the magician with the system. The system is divided into five phases.

Phase One: The eight colours
Phase Two: The four elements
Phase Three: Duality
Phase Four: The Cybermorphic Level of Octarine
Phase Five: A Total Immersion into Chaos.

Phase One: The Eight Colours

Universal requirements
i)   Keep a Diary of everything you do.
ii)   A basic level of meditation and visualisation
iii)   Knowledge of a sigil creation method
iv)   Knowledge of a mantra creation method
v)   Perseverance

Psyche Magic
Visualisation:
Sit still and breath slowly but regularly. Create a scene in your imagination of a place you associate with psyche, the deep mind, and your subconscious. Visualise this place regularly. Make notes on how you feel after visiting this place, what kinds of things you visualise, anything that seems out of place, any illumination you receive. What does it all tell you about your attitudes towards your inner self? What have you suppressed down there? What inner motivations and drives are there? Which ones are useful to you? Can you enhance them? Which ones cause you problems? Can

they be changed to work to your advantage? Can they be replaced? What inner drives and motivations do you feel you need but don't have? What is psyche anyway?

Sorcery:
What can you do to improve it? Use sorcery to aid mundane means. Does it work? Has it improved the situation? Has it made it worse? If so, is the magic to blame or your misguided intent? Do you need to reflect more on the situation before proceeding? What kinds of sorcery do you find works best for this? Sigils? Mantras? Servitors? Sympathetic magic? Visualisations?

Magical Artefact creation:
Make a magical artefact that represents psyche. A good example might be a mandala. Evoke the spirit by staring intently at the mandala whilst in meditation either in or out of ritual.

Philosophy and Mythology:
What magical and cosmological systems are you aware of? What is the role of Psyche in these systems? How much have these views influenced your ideas on psyche? How much have other societal and peer pressures influenced you? Where do these ideas agree and disagree? Which ones make more sense to you?

Ego Magic

Visualisation:
Sit still and breath slowly but regularly. Create a scene in your imagination of a place you associate with pride, charisma, leadership and personas. Visualise this place regularly. Make notes on how you feel after visiting this place, what kinds of things you visualise, anything that seems out of place, any illumination you receive. What does it all tell you about how others perceive you? How well do you wear the masks of your various personae? How well do you present yourself in your different social circles? How dominant/submissive are you in these roles? Are you comfortable with these roles? Is there a way to change any of them? What is ego anyway?

Sorcery:
What can you do to improve it? Use sorcery to aid mundane means. Does it work? Has it improved the situation? Has it made it worse? If so, is the magic to blame or your misguided intent? Do you need to reflect more on the situation before proceeding? What kinds of sorcery do you find works best for this? Sigils? Mantras? Servitors? Sympathetic magic? Visualisations?

Magical Artefact creation:
Make a magical artefact that represents ego. A good example might be a mask. In this example you may obtain a beautiful mask and paint it yellow/gold and adorn it with sigil like patterns. Invoke the spirit by wearing the mask and becoming the 'ego magic' persona to work your ego spells, either in or out of ritual.

Philosophy and Mythology:
What magical and cosmological systems are you aware of? What is the role of Ego in these systems? How much have these views influenced your ideas on ego? How much have other societal and peer pressures influenced you? Where do these ideas agree and disagree? Which ones make more sense to you?

Play Magic

Visualisation:
Sit still and breath slowly but regularly. Create a scene in your imagination of a place you associate with play, fun, and pleasure. Visualise this place regularly. Make notes on how you feel after visiting this place, what kinds of things you visualise, anything that seems out of place, any illumination you receive. What does it all tell you about the way you enjoy pleasures? What repressed desires for pleasure do you have? Are your pleasurable activities really pleasurable to you or do you just do them because they are 'meant to be fun'? Do you follow your own desires or other peoples? How well do you learn to see the fun even in a bad situation? How well do you utilise your time and resources for fun and pleasure? Can this be improved? How do you define play?

Sorcery:
What can you do to improve it? Use sorcery to aid mundane means. Does it work? Has it improved the situation? Has it made it worse? If so, is the magic to blame or your misguided intent? Do you need to reflect more on the situation before proceeding? What kinds of sorcery do you find works best for this? Sigils? Mantras? Servitors? Sympathetic magic? Visualisations?

Magical Artefact creation:
Make a magical artefact that represents play. A good example might be a toy. In this example you may obtain a toy and paint/sew a blue sigil on it. Evoke the spirit by playing with the toy either in or out of ritual.

Philosophy and Mythology:
What magickal and cosmological systems are you aware of? What is the role of Play in these systems? How much have these views influenced your ideas on play? How much have other societal and peer pressures influenced you? Where do these ideas agree and disagree? Which ones make more sense to you?

Work Magic

Visualisation:

Sit still and breath slowly but regularly. Create a scene in your imagination of a place you associate with work, effort, and gathering resources. Visualise this place regularly. Make notes on how you feel after visiting this place, what kinds of things you visualise, anything that seems out of place, any illumination you receive. What does it all tell you about how efficiently you gather resources? Are you gathering enough? Are you working too hard for too little reward? Do you enjoy your work? Is there something you could do for a living that you would enjoy better? If not, could you get training for something that would? What does work mean to you?

Sorcery:

What can you do to improve it? Use sorcery to aid mundane means. Does it work? Has it improved the situation? Has it made it worse? If so, is the magic to blame or your misguided intent? Do you need to reflect more on the situation before proceeding? What kinds of sorcery do you find works best for this? Sigils? Mantras? Servitors? Sympathetic magic? Visualisations?

Magical Artefact creation:

Make a magical artefact that represents work. A good example might be a tool. In this example you may obtain a tool and paint it with an orange/grey sigil. Evoke the spirit by pretending to work with the tool, either in or out of ritual.

Philosophy and Mythology:

What magical and cosmological systems are you aware of? What is the role of Work in these systems? How much have these views influenced your ideas on work? How much have other societal and peer pressures influenced you? Where do these ideas agree and disagree? Which ones make more sense to you?

Death Magic

Visualisation:

Sit still and breath slowly but regularly. Create a scene in your imagination of a place you associate with death, release, entropy and decay. Visualise this place regularly. Make notes on how you feel after visiting this place, what kinds of things you visualise, anything that seems out of place, any illumination you receive. What does it all tell you about your attitudes towards death? Your ability to release things no longer needed in your life? How do you manage release, do you donate things you don't need to those who might? Dump in recycling or the trash? Do you hoard? How well do you cope when loved ones die, or something breaks that holds sentimental value? Are you prepared for your own death? What do you believe happens when you die? What do you think death is exactly?

Sorcery:

What can you do to improve it? Use sorcery to aid mundane means. Does it work? Has it improved the situation? Has it made it worse? If so, is the magic to blame or your misguided intent? Do you need to reflect more on the situation before proceeding? What kinds of sorcery do you find works best for this? Sigils? Mantras? Servitors? Sympathetic magic? Visualisations?

Magical Artefact creation:

Make a magical artefact that represents death. A good example might be to bundle together old bits of waste from your home. In this example you may obtain some chicken bones, some old wire and bits of lead (the metal of Saturn, the planet of Death) and tie it with black string or thread. Evoke the spirit burning thirteen black candles arranged around the artefact either in or out of ritual.

Philosophy and Mythology:

What magical and cosmological systems are you aware of? What is the role of Death in these systems? How much have these

164

views influenced your ideas on death? How much have other societal and peer pressures influenced you? Where do these ideas agree and disagree? Which ones make more sense to you?

Sex Magic

Visualisation:

Sit still and breath slowly but regularly. Create a scene in your imagination of a place you associate with sex, creativity, and fertility. Before continuing stand up and begin to sway gently in rhythmical serpentine motions. Re-visualise the place whilst continuing to sway seductively. Visualise this place regularly. Make notes on how you feel after visiting this place, what kinds of things you visualise, anything that seems out of place, any illumination you receive. What does it all tell you about the state of your creativity? What repressed creative impulses need a release? Do you enjoy your current creative outlets, or do you have enough? Would you be better creating something new and fresh? How fertile is your world? Do you grow plants? Breed animals? Have children? If you have children, how well are you stimulating their creative minds? Are you trying to reduce the risk of pregnancy? If so are you directing your creative impulses elsewhere (presuming you are already using an effective contraceptive)? What is sex?

Sorcery:

What can you do to improve it? Use sorcery to aid mundane means. Does it work? Has it improved the situation? Has it made it worse? If so, is the magic to blame or your misguided intent? Do you need to reflect more on the situation before proceeding? What kinds of sorcery do you find works best for this? Sigils? Mantras? Servitors? Sympathetic magic? Visualisations?

Magical Artefact creation:

Make a magical artefact that represents sex. A good example might be a paint brush kept in a pot. The pot symbolises the female sexual organ and the brush the male. In this example you may obtain the brush and pot and paint them with purple/silver sigils. Evoke the spirit by taking some paint and some paper and making wild brush strokes to create wild and abstract painting that sigilises your intent. Do this either in or out of ritual.

Philosophy and Mythology:

What magical and cosmological systems are you aware of? What is the role of Sex in these systems? How much have these views influenced your ideas on sex? How much have other societal and peer pressures influenced you? Where do these ideas agree and disagree? Which ones make more sense to you?

War Magic

Visualisation:

Sit still and breath slowly but regularly. Create a scene in your imagination of a place you associate with war, conflict and threat. Now before continuing stand up and assume a fighting posture. Keep visualising yourself in the place of war. As you move in the place you visualise, move into other aggressive stances, moving slowly and gently. It helps if you have practised martial arts, but this isn't necessary, just move slowly and gently with grace. Visualise this place regularly. Make notes on how you feel after visiting this place, what kinds of things you visualise, anything that seems out of place, any illumination you receive. What does it all tell you about how well you stand up for yourself? How much of the conflict is ill directed and how much of it would be better dealt with in other ways? Who is invading your space without you standing up for yourself? What situations are there where it is better to run away and survive to fight another day? What does war mean?

Sorcery:

What can you do to improve it? Use sorcery to aid mundane means. Does it work? Has it improved the situation? Has it made it worse? If so, is the magic to blame or your misguided intent? Do you need to reflect more on the situation before proceeding? What kinds of sorcery do you find works best for

this? Sigils? Mantras? Servitors? Sympathetic magic?
Visualisations?

Magical Artefact creation:

Make a magical artefact that represents war. A good example
might be a weapon. In this example you may obtain a weapon
and paint on it a red sigil of war, the symbol of mars and
appropriate runes, and evoke the spirit by smiting imaginary
enemies with the weapon, either in or out of ritual.

Philosophy and Mythology:

What magical and cosmological systems are you aware of? What
is the role of War in these systems? How much have these views
influenced your ideas on war? How much have other societal and
peer pressures influenced you? Where do these ideas agree and
disagree? Which ones make more sense to you?

Love Magic
Visualisation:

Sit still and breath slowly but regularly. Create a scene in your
imagination of a place you associate with love and friendship.
Somewhere you feel secure, happy and safe. Visualise this place
regularly. Make notes on how you feel after visiting this place,
what kinds of things you visualise, anything that seems out of
place, any illumination you receive. What does it all tell you
about the state of your love life and friendships? How much do
you practise self-love? Can you improve any of this? What is love
anyway?

Sorcery:

What can you do to improve it? Use sorcery to aid mundane
means. Does it work? Has it improved the situation? Has it
made it worse? If so, is the magic to blame or your misguided
intent? Do you need to reflect more on the situation before
proceeding? What kinds of sorcery do you find works best for
this? Sigils? Mantras? Servitors? Sympathetic magic?
Visualisations?

Magical Artefact creation:
Make a magical artefact that represents love. A good example might be a cuddly toy. In this example you may obtain a suitable teddy or other cuddly toy, and apply a green ribbon, bow or other piece of clothing, sew a sigil into the fabric, and evoke the spirit by cuddling the toy, either in or out of ritual.

Philosophy and Mythology:
What magical and cosmological systems are you aware of? What is the role of Love in these systems? How much have these views influenced your ideas on love? How much have other societal and peer pressures influenced you? Where do these ideas agree and disagree? Which ones make more sense to you?

Additional Exercises
What other systems based on the number eight do you know? How do they fit with this system? Do they fit with this system? What has this system missed out that is included in the other and vice-versa? Or are they just completely different?

Phase Two: The Four Elements

Universal requirements
i) Keep a Diary of everything you do.
ii) An intermediate level of meditation and visualisation
iii) Knowledge and practise in servitor/daemon creation/summoning, their control and banishing.
iv) Knowledge of the four magical operations (divination, invocation, evocation and enchantment)
v) Study of the meanings and relationships of the four classical elements

Fire Magic
Visualisation:
Sit still and breath slowly but regularly. Create a scene in your imagination of a place made entirely of Fire. Are there buildings? What kind of beings or creatures inhabit this place? Can you talk to them? What do they say to you? How do they behave? Make notes of all your communications with these entities and their reactions to you.

Elemental:
Using the knowledge of these entities gained in visualisation, find an appropriate time to make use of their energy in a ritual. Make notes on how successful this summoning was and how successful the results were. Do this as many times as it takes to achieve reasonable success.

Sword of Invocation:
Make or obtain a sword, or a magical artefact that you may use as a magical weapon to symbolise the operation of invocation (allowing your conscious mind to be controlled by an intelligence/being or entity such as a Deity/hero/character from mythology, fiction or history.) Make notes on how it feels to be any identities other than 'your own'. What does it tell you about the nature of 'your identity'? Did the invocation give you the results you desired?

Earth Magic

Visualisation:

Sit still and breath slowly but regularly. Create a scene in your imagination of a place made entirely of Earth. What kind of creatures and beings live in it and how do they interact with one another? Can you talk to them? What do they say? How do they treat you and behave towards your presence? Make notes of your experiences in this place.

Elemental:

Using the knowledge you have gained of these beings, find a good time to make use of their qualities in a spell and attempt to summon one to aid your intent. Make notes on the success or otherwise of your contact and the success of the results in achieving your intent. Repeat this exercise as many times as it takes to achieve reasonable success.

Pentacle/Disc of Evocation:

Make or obtain a disc or pentacle, or a magical artefact that you may use to symbolise the magical operation of evocation, (the summoning into physical space the presence of a spirit/entity/servitor/elemental or even a deity). Make notes on the success of any operations performed with this tool.

Air Magic

Visualisation:

Sit still and breath slowly but regularly. Create a scene in your imagination of a place made entirely of Air. What is it like? What kind of creatures and beings live in this place? How do they behave and interact with one another? What are their relationships? Can you talk to them? What kind of things do they say and how do they treat you? Make notes of your experiences in this place.

Elemental:

Using the knowledge you have gained of these beings, attempt to summon one to aid you in a ritual of appropriate intent. Make notes on how successful you felt the summoning to be, and the success or otherwise of your intents. Repeat this exercise as many times as it takes to gain reasonable results.

Wand/Staff of Enchantment:
Make or obtain a wand or staff, or other magical artefact that you may use to represent the magical operation of enchantment. (The casting of a spell to bring about the direct manifestation of an intent). Use this to aid you in workings of enchantment and make notes of your success or otherwise when using this weapon.

Water Magic

Visualisation:
Sit still and breath slowly but regularly. Create a scene in your imagination of a place made entirely of Water. What are the beings and creatures that inhabit this place like? In what way do they relate to one another? Can you communicate with them? How do they react to you and what if anything do they say to you? Make notes of your experiences in this place.

Elemental:
Using the knowledge you have gained from your contact with these entities, summon one to aid you in a ritual that you feel has an intent they can help you with. Makes notes on the success of your contact and the success or otherwise in achieving a result that matches your intent. Repeat this exercise as many times as it takes to achieve reasonable success.

Cup of Divination:
Make or obtain a 'Cup' or other magical weapon that can symbolise the operation of divination. Use this to aid your divinations and the practise of different divination methods. Make notes on the success and failures of the divinations you have made with the aid of this weapon.

Additional Exercises

1) What other systems based on the number four do you know? How do they fit with this system? Do they fit with this system? What has this system missed out that is included in the other and vice-versa? Or are they just completely different?

2) In the Cybermorphic Kaosphere Model, Fire is identity, Earth is resources, Air is separation and Water is unification. How well does this fit with your experience of the elementals?

3) In Carroll's 'Liber Kaos', Fire is energy, Earth is mass, Air is space and Water is time. How well does this fit with your experience of the elementals? If you visualise entities and places made of Energy, Mass, Space and Time, do they behave differently than the classical elementals? How different are they?

4) Traditionally, spirits of these elements have been called to guard quarters in magical rituals. Practise this in your own way and record how effective you think it is. Try the elements in various orders and in different directions (i.e. Clockwise, Anticlockwise and Crossways). What difference does this make?

5) A Tarot deck is a kind of magical Swiss army knife and can be used for enchantment, divination, evocation and invocation. Try each of these operations using Tarot and record your levels of success. (Instead of Tarot you may use Rune Stones, I-Ching or some other preferred tool you think is capable of being used for all four operations).

Phase Three: Duality

Universal requirements
i) Keep a Diary of everything you do.
ii) An experienced level of meditation and visualisation
iii) Proficient level of attainment on all previous levels of this system

Doing Magic
Pathworking Meditation
Your level of visualisation should be of dreamlike quality at this stage. You should also be able to lead pathworkings, both prepared and spontaneously. You should also be capable of integrating pathworkings into a ritual structure, and even involving movement on the parts of the participants.

Excitatory Gnosis
You should be familiar with the use of excitatory forms of gnosis in ritual, such as orgasm, arrogance, anger and joy. Other methods might include spinning, dancing and martial arts.

Magical Power and Control
How much power do you have over your own life situation? In what ways can you acquire more? Would it be worth the effort? Are you able to enjoy the fruits of power you currently wield? If not, what is stopping you?

Being Magic
Stillness Meditation
You should be able not only to stay still for a length of time in various positions, but also to still the mind and think of nothing. Control of breathing rhythms can help in this.

Inhibitory Gnosis
You should be familiar with the use of inhibitory forms of gnosis in ritual, such as release, humiliation, rapture and terror. Other

methods might include hyperventilation, bondage or intoxication.

Mystical Balance and Ecstasy
Are you able to enjoy all aspects of your life? Do you have safe spaces where you can stop controlling, sit back and enjoy the ride? Do you have the power to acquire more? If not, are you blocking yourself or is something external stopping you?

Additional Exercises
1) What other systems of duality do you know? How do they fit with this system? Do they fit with this system? What has this system missed out that is included in the other and vice-versa? Or are they just completely different?

2) In the Cybermorphic Kaosphere Model, Being is meant to correspond to Salt, Objects, Particles, Norse Ice and the 'yin' principle and Doing is meant to correspond to Sulphur, Processes, Waves, Norse Fire and the 'yang' principle. How well does this fit with your experience of these descriptions of duality?

Phase Four:
The Cybermorphic Level of Octarine

Pure Magic
Illumination
You should be familiar with what illumination really means by now. Also, you should be capable of getting illumination from all sorts of seemingly mundane information.

Aura Magic
At this stage you should be adept at spontaneous aura manipulation, you should be able to use it for healing, grounding, protection and telepathy. There are many other uses for Aura magic, and you should become familiar with what they are, and gain some experience in them. You should be able to gain such knowledge yourself using the skills you have developed so far.

The Balance of Balance and Imbalance
How well does duality flow within you? Are you enjoying as good a relationship with light as the dark? Or vice versa? Are you at home with being as much as doing? Or vice versa? Does the Hermaphrodite dance within you? Is your Anima/Animus allowed the freedom to express itself as it wishes? At this level, your whole self must be one. There is no room for suppression. Even balance itself must be balanced with imbalance. In this way you may learn to 'walk forwards' in the spiritual sense. Balance on its own is merely standing still...

Thoughts on Pure Magic
Pure Magic is said to correspond to Ether, Mercury, Uranus, Octarine, Hermaphrodite, Baphomet, Wyrd, the Tao, Leary's Eighth Circuit, Quantum Consciousness and to Information itself.
  How does this sit with your thoughts and experiences of these things? What other correspondences can you think of? How well does Pure Magic combine with Being and Doing to form a system of threes? How well does it combine with the four elements to

form a system of fives? How well does it combine with the eight colours to form a system of nines?

Phase Five: A Total Immersion into Chaos.

Chaos Magic
Infinite Possibility

It is time to enter into that realm where all possibilities are true, the Chaos Unmanifest itself. Here no system is true, and you can leave the crutches of the Cybermorphic Kaosphere and any other cosmological map behind you. From here you can create your own reality and your own magical system, which you may like to put in writing and share with others like I have done or you may keep it to yourself. There is no truth here, and you are permitted to do everything you desire. Just be careful not to desire your own destruction.

To stay here for too long is to invite madness, but to return often is to invigorate the mind with fresh inspiration. When you return to duality, you may still use old systems you have left behind. I mean why not? Nothing is stopping you. But the thing is you simply don't need to. Unless you get out of practise, or need to work in a group where not everyone can do without the props. And besides, it can still be fun to use toys even when we've 'outgrown' them!

To reach the Chaos Unmanifest you must use all the skills that you have learned in the previous four phases. If you cannot work out how to do it for yourself, then you are not yet ready. This is the final test of this training system.

Appendix D

Divination

Divination using the Cybermorphic Kaosphere system is both simple and in my experience quite effective. The basic description below is one I use with a Tarot deck, although I am sure you are probably capable of adapting it to your own preferred system.

Tarot method

After giving the deck a good shuffle, cut the deck in two. Place the smallest pile on '0' and the largest pile on '1'. Cut the pile on '1' leaving the bottom pile where it is and moving the top pile to '2'. Cut pile '1' again in the same way putting the cards removed on '3'. Then cut '2' in the same way putting the cards on '4'. Now cut '1' again putting the cards on '5'. Cut '2' putting the cards on '6'. Cut '3' putting the cards on '7'. Finally cut '4' putting the cards on '8'. You should now have nine piles arranged about in the form of a chaosphere. Turn over the top cards and interpret them according to the position they are in...

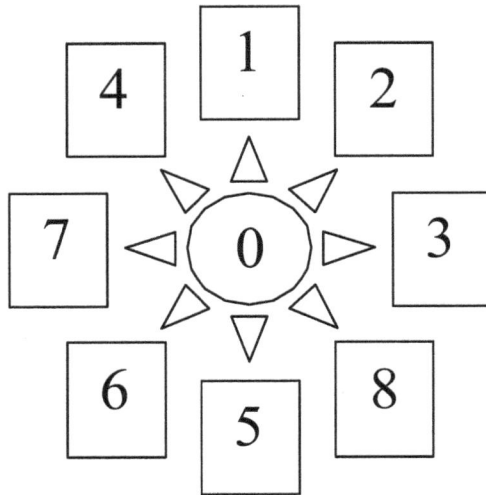

0. Octarine. Magic, control and probabilities about to manifest. (If needed look at the bottom card of this pile for the Chaos Unmanifest, which represents hidden possibility, ecstasy and going with the flow.)

1. Psyche. The inner hidden self of the problem/Querent.

2. Death. Entropy, decay, things coming to an end.

3. Play. Pleasure and leisure influences.

4. War. Forces of opposition, resistance, enemies or hostile threat.

5. Ego. Outward expression of the problem/Querent.

6. Sex. Creative forces, things about to begin.

7. Work. Where some effort needs to be applied, stress.

8. Love. Forces of co-operation, alliance, partnership, friends and even romance.

Coin Method

Using the coin method you can draw six lines, either broken or unbroken. You do this once for a simple answer, or you can do it 9 times (one for each of the positions mentioned in the Tarot method) for an in depth answer. Simply, for each set of six lines toss a coin six times. Starting from the bottom and working up, if the coin is a head draw an unbroken line, else draw a broken line.

The first three lines indicate the past, present and future. A broken line indicates Chaos Unmanifest, things that exist in potential, infinite possibility and things that are manifesting outside the control of the Querent.

An unbroken line represents Ether, Mercury, Octarine forces, and things that are caused by, or are under the control of the Querent.

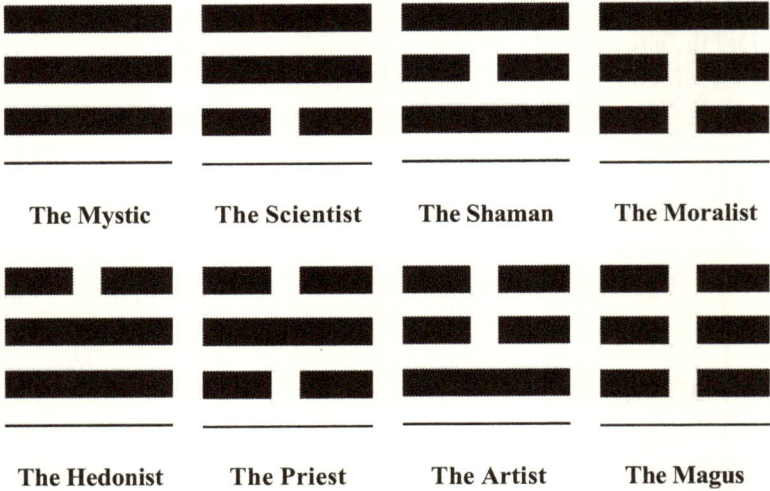

The Mystic	The Scientist	The Shaman	The Moralist

The Hedonist	The Priest	The Artist	The Magus

The Mystic represents going with the flow. The Scientist attempts to create order where there was none. The Shaman attempts to control the present using past and future chaos. The Moralist attempts to maintain established orders. The Hedonist attempts to maintain established pleasures. The Priest looks to past and future order at the neglect of the present. The Artist tries to find beauty and freedom with in order. The Magus is in the position of ultimate control.

The next three lines build another trigram (completing the hexagram) which form one of the eight colours. In this trigram an unbroken line represents doing, whilst a broken line represents being. These are drawn on top of the previous trigram to form one of sixty-four hexagrams.

These may look the same as the traditional I-Ching, but differ greatly in meaning.

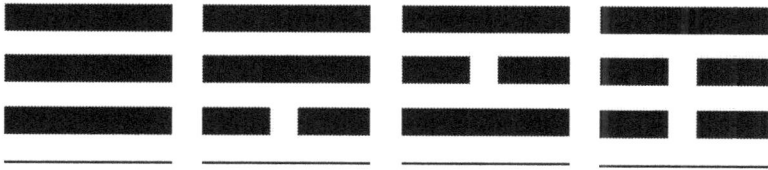

| Psyche | Ego | Play | Work |

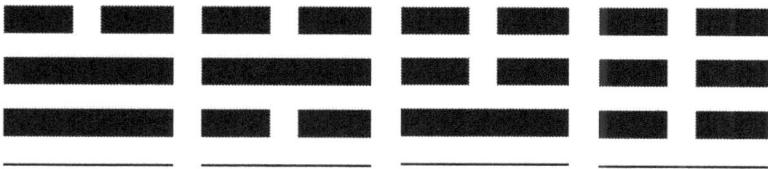

| Death | Sex | War | Love |

Appendix E

Ugemaaph
(Also known as Kaobala or the Chaos Ygg)

Notice how the opposing sides of the tree combine to form complimentary forces. Our Identity comes from what we decide to Unite ourselves with. Resources are what we have Separated (Divided) from ourselves. The more we know our inner Psyche, the greater our capacity for Love. The greater our Personality (Ego), the better we are at protecting the things important to us (War). The more efficient our Work, the better able we are to

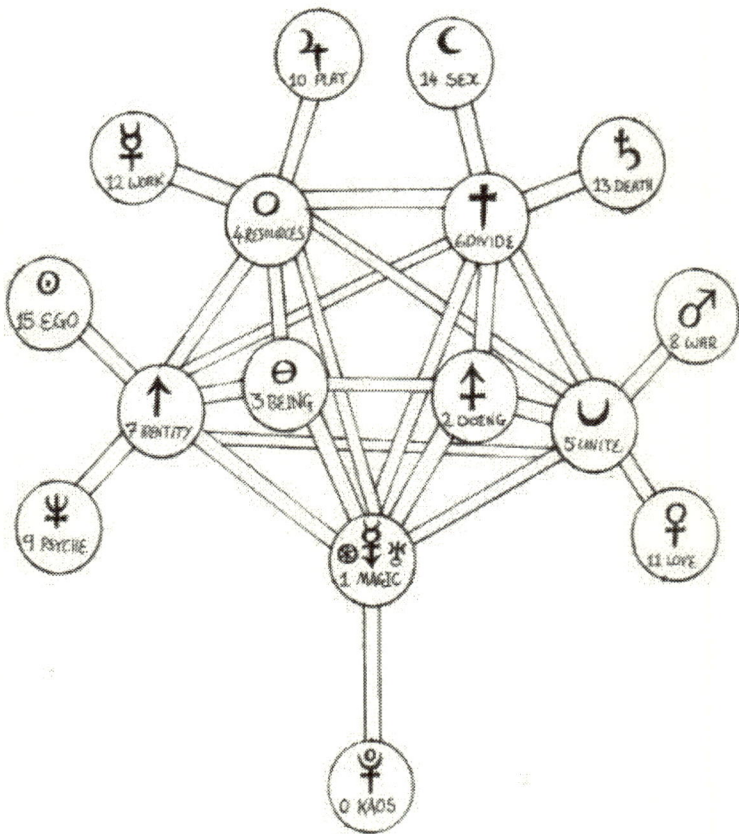

10 PLAY

14 SEX

12 WORK

4 RESOURCES

6 DIVIDE

13 DEATH

15 EGO

3 BEING

2 DOING

8 WAR

7 IDENTITY

5 UNITE

9 PSYCHE

1 MAGIC

11 LOVE

0 KAOS

release from ourselves what we no longer need (Death). The more we stimulate our creativity (Sex), the more we can enjoy life (Play). These pairs may also combine in destructive, less helpful ways...

Glossary

Aeon
A period of space time in which consciousness is within a particular generalized state. Systems of Aeonics often represent a scale of progression through various states or stages of the collective human consciousness. In practice the older aeons never actually get left behind entirely, they simply become the foundation or building blocks of the next aeon. Many still cling to older aeons, for better or worse.

Aether
The boundary or gateway between the illusory existence we call 'reality' and the infinite non-existence one might be tempted to call the Chaos Unmanifest. Has also been known as Kia, Mercury, Tao, Christ, Chi and many other names, some anthropomorphic, others abstract.

Being
The concept or illusion of things having something fixed about them. The idea that things are objects. In a more abstract sense, something's 'being' simply refers to the data or information that currently describes that object.

Butterfly Effect
A concept from Chaos Mathematics, or Non-Linear Dynamics, that shows how small changes in initial conditions can result in large differences over a distance of space time. Although science has no way of predicting which way those long term differences will go, this has not stopped magicians from using the theory in their magics.

Chaos (Kaos and Khaos)
The source of creation in Greek mythology. Has since been used by various theologians, sorcerers, alchemists, magicians and scientists in their theories. It has also erroneously become

184

associated with 'disorder'. Chaos is neither disorder nor order. In this book three spellings of Chaos will be found. 'Chaos' is the more general spelling that will be found throughout the book. 'Kaos' will be used specifically when discussing a particular aspect of my own system of alchemy. Finally, it is spelled as 'Khaos' in a quote from Deadlock from the ABC Warriors. I have kept Pat Mills spelling in order to be faithful to the original text I have taken the quote from.

Chaos Unmanifest
An attempt to see Chaos as a source of existence, without making it primal or primordial. In other words a breaking free of the chains of linear time based creation, that would posit Chaos as a kind of monotheistic creator, and see it rather as something that is continually manifesting in space time at all points simultaneously.

Demon (Daemon and Servitor)
A spirit that in some way serves or obeys the command of a magician. These may be externalized parts of the magicians psyche, or they may entities found in nature, or called up from some 'other' place or plane of existence.

Doing
The concept or illusion that 'all is change'.

Elemental
Of the elements. Often used to mean spirits that are of the elements. The elements traditionally being seen as Earth, Air, Fire and Water.

Fractal
A construct from Chaos Mathematics which exhibits a geometry that appears to occupy a partial dimension. They usually have an infinitely detailed structure bound within the finite.

Gnosis
Knowledge. Originally from the Gnostic Luciferian tradition and meant the spiritual knowledge gained from eating fruit from the

tree of the 'Knowledge of Good and Evil', which freed us from our enslavement in the garden of Eden, where mankind had been trapped by the demiurge. When the fruit was eaten, mankind's eyes were opened, meaning our spiritual eyes. In modern times, the attainment of Gnosis has come to mean something like Illumination.

Illumination
A state in which a spiritual light is cast, revealing things that before lay hidden in the spiritual darkness. Alternatively this may refer to seeing the spiritual light that is always there but which we blocked out by not opening our spiritual eyes. In a more general sense is connected to spiritual revelations gained through various methods.

Kia
A term used by Spare which may be interpreted as referring to that part of the Aether which is of direct personal significance to the individual.

Mercury
The alchemical principle that represents the idea of 'Transcending the duality between Being and Doing' (Which Alchemists called Salt and Sulphur). Associated with the idea of Aether, Kia and Octarine. Also relevant to Gnosis and Illumination. Not to be confused with planetary mercury.

Octarine
The colour of magic. From the disk world novels of Terry Pratchett. First used in magic by Carroll. The idea that Aether has a colour all of its own that is only visible to those who have achieved Gnosis, gained Illumination or have opened 'their spiritual eye'.

Results Magic
Bringing about measurable material results with magical power. The idea that only by observable and verifiable results can we measure how much progress we are making in our magical

studies.

Salt
The alchemical principle that represents the idea of 'Being'.

Sigil
A glyph charged with magical intent.

Strange Attractor
A concept from Chaos Mathematics. Something which, left to its own devices, tends towards a state that, although existing within certain finite bounds, is always changing and never repeats itself.

Sulphur
The alchemical principle that represents the idea of 'Doing'.

Thelema
A religion or magical movement started by Crowley, based on his channeled "Book of the Law". The name means 'Will' and its most famous motto is "Do what thou Wilt shall be the whole of the Law. Love is the Law, Love under Will."

Witchcraft
The name given to magic in folk tradition throughout the world by Europeans. This has created an artificial and illusory divide between folk magic and magic thought to belong to the 'educated classes'. In modern times there has also been an unfortunate attempt to steal the term for a neo-pagan religion made up by Gerald Gardener and which is really just a watered down version of Thelema. Witchcraft before Gardener was not a religion and never had been.

Bibliography

References

Brewster, Charles *Liber Cyber* UK: self-published, 1991.

Carroll, Peter J. *Liber Kaos* York Beach, ME, U.S.A.: Samuel Weiser, Inc., 1992.

Carroll, Peter J. *Liber Null & Psychonaut* York Beach, ME, U.S.A.: Samuel Weiser, Inc., 1987.

Carroll, Peter J. *PsyberMagick* Temp, AZ, U.S.A.: New Falcon Publications, 1997.

Crowley, Aliester *The Book of Thoth* York Beach, ME, U.S.A.: Samuel Weiser, Inc., 1993.

Davies, Nigel *The Aztecs* London, U.K.: The Folio Society, 2000.

Dee, John *The Hieroglyphic Monad* tr. J. W. Hamilton-Jones, London, U.K., 1947.

Defenestrate-Bascule, Orryelle *Emit fo yrotsreH feirB A* Vict., Australia: Inspiral Multimedia Press, 2003.

Dukes, Ramsey *Words Made Flesh* Winchester, U.K.: The Mouse That Spins, 1988.

Dukes, Ramsey *What I did in My Holidays* Winchester, U.K.: The Mouse That Spins, 1998.

Evola, Julius *The Hermetic Tradition* Rochester, VT, U.S.A.: Inner Traditions International, 1995.

Fries, Jan *Living Midnight* Oxford, U.K.: Mandrake of Oxford, 1998.

Fries, Jan *Helrunar* Oxford, U.K.: Mandrake of Oxford, 1997.

Fries, Jan *Seidways* Oxford, U.K.: Mandrake of Oxford, 1996.

Fries, Jan *Visual Magick* Oxford, U.K.: Mandrake of Oxford, 1992.

Gibran, Kahlil *The Prophet* London, U.K.: Penguin, 1992.

Gleick, James *Chaos: Making a New Science* London, U.K.: Abacus, 1995.

Harris, Nathaniel J. *Witcha: A Book of Cunning* Norwich, U.K.: self-published, 2002.

Hawkins, Jaq D. *Spirits of the Earth* Chieveley, U.K.: Capall Bann, 1998.

Hawkins, Jaq D. *Spirits of the Air* Chieveley, U.K.: Capall Bann, 1998.

Hawkins, Jaq D. *Spirits of the Fire* Chieveley, U.K.: Capall Bann, 1999.

Hawkins, Jaq D. *Spirits of the Water* Chieveley, U.K.: Capall Bann, 2000.

Hawkins, Jaq D. *Spirits of the Aether* Chieveley, U.K.: Capall

Bann, 2001.

Hawkins, Jaq D. *The Chaos Monkey* Chieveley, U.K.: Capall Bann, 2002.

Hawkins, Jaq D. *Understanding Chaos Magic* Chieveley, U.K.: Capall Bann, 1996.

Hine, Phil *Condensed Chaos* Tempe, AZ, U.S.A.: New Falcon Publications, 1996.

Hutin, Serge *A History of Alchemy* tr. Tamara Alferoff New York, NY, U.S.A.: Tower Publications, Inc. 1962.

Leary, Timothy *Info-Psychology* Phoenix, AZ, U.S.A.: New Falcon Publications, 1994.

Lee, Dave *Chaotopia!* Leeds, U.K.: Attractor, 1997.

Lovecraft, H. P. *Omnibus 2: Dagon and Other Macabre Tales* London, U.K.: Harper Collins Publishers, 1994.

Meeuwissen, Tony *The Key to the Kingdom* London, U.K.: Pavilion Books Limited, 1992.

Mills, Pat & Tony Skinner *ABC Warriors – Khronicles of Khaos & Hellbringer* London, U.K.: Hamlyn, 1997.

Moorcock, Michael *Phoenix in Obsidian* St. Albans, U.K.: Mayflower, 1974.

Moorcock, Michael *The End of dl Songs* St. Albans, U.K.: Mayflower, 1977.

Moorcock, Michael *The Knight of the Swords* St. Albans, U.K.: Mayflower, 1981.

Moorcock, Michael *The Quest for Tanelorn* St. Albans, U.K.: Mayflower, 1975.

Nema *Maat Magick* Oxford, U.K.: Mandrake of Oxford, 1995

Nema *Maat Magick and Chaos Magick* Brighton, U.K.: *Razor Smile Issue One*, 2002.

Roberts, J.M. *Prehistory and the First Civilizations* London, U.K.: Duncan Baird Publishers, 1999.

Roob, Alexander *Alchemy and Mysticism* Koln, Germany: Benedikt Taschen Verlag, 2001.

Shah, Idries *The Way of the Sufi* London, U.K.: Penguin Arkana, 1990.

Spare, Austin Osman *Earth Inferno* London, U.K.: Co-operative Printing Society, 1905.

Spare, Austin Osman *The Book of Pleasure (Self-Love)* London, U.K.: Co-operative Printing Society, 1913.

Tzu, Sun *The New Translation (The Art of War)* tr. J. H. Huang New York, NY, U.S.A.: Harper, 1993.

Willis, Tony *Discover Runes* London, U.K.: 1986.

Wilson, Robert Anton & Robert Shea *The Illuminatus! Trilogy* London, U.K.: Raven Books, 1998.

Wilson, Robert Anton *Prometheus Rising* Tempe, AZ, U.S.A.:
New Falcon Publications, 1999.

Younger, Malaclypse the *Principia Discordia* San Francisco, CA,
U.S.A.: POEE Head Temple, 1970.

193

194

196

Contact KIA

KIA
Kaotic Illuminated
Adepts

http://www.kiamagic.com/kia/

KIA is an international networking organisation for Chaos Magicians who want to work in groups and/or solo, having contact and communication with other groups and/or solo magicians. It is non-hierarchical, non-graded, non-initiation and non-payment based and works on the following core principles:

*1. No Hierarchy whatsoever, any initiation is optional and based on individual requirements as there are no grades of any kind, no dues and absolutely **NO** obligation.*

2. Everyone is entitled to a full members list (to make this possible a minimum amount of contact details should be provided, of email, town/city and country. Postal Address and/or Phone number optional unless no email address provided). Post Boxes with Aliases are fine.

3. Any member is free to invite/exclude any other member to anything they personally organise. Those that organise a meeting may invite non-members, however this should be made clear to members who are also invited.

4. Any member may leave whenever they want, although no-one may ever be forced to leave. It is enough that members you don't personally like won't be invited to things you don't want them to be.

5. It is our wish that this structure will make for an individualistic, non-hierarchical organisation, capable of forming meetings on local, national and international levels within a few years to a decade.

If you are interested in membership, apply via our website…